General editor
Peter
Herriot

New
Essential
Psychology

Memory,
Thinking
and
Language

ALREADY PUBLISHED IN THIS SERIES

Applying Psychology in Organizations
Frank Blackler and Sylvia Shimmin

Cognitive Development and Education
Johanna Turner

Experimental Design and Statistics
Second edition
Steve Miller

Individual Differences
Vivian Shackleton and Clive Fletcher

Instinct, Environment and Behaviour
S.E.G. Lea

Learning Theory and Behaviour Modification
Stephen Walker

Personality Theory and Clinical Practice
Peter Fonagy and Anna Higgitt

Selves in Relation
An introduction to psychotherapy and groups
Keith Oatley

Social Interaction and its Management
Judy Gahagan

FORTHCOMING TITLES IN THE SERIES

Attitudes and Decisions
J. Richard Eiser and Joop van der Pligt

Human Physiological Psychology
Tony Gale

Multivariate Design and Statistics
Steve Miller

Judith Greene

Memory, Thinking and Language

Topics in cognitive psychology

Methuen

London and New York

First published in 1987 by
Methuen & Co. Ltd
11 New Fetter Lane, London EC4P 4EE

© 1987 Judith Greene

Typeset by Hope Services
Abingdon, Oxon
Printed and bound in Great Britain by
Richard Clay Ltd, Bungay, Suffolk

British Library Cataloguing in Publication
Data

Greene, Judith
Memory, thinking and language:
topics in cognitive psychology.
– (New essential psychology).
1. Cognition
I. Title   II. Greene, Judith. Thinking
and language   III. Series
155.4'13   BF311
ISBN 0–416–33800–3

To the 3 Js, Janet, John and Jonathan
from the 4th J

Contents

1   Introduction   1
2   Thinking and knowledge   6
3   The structure of knowledge   17
4   Active memory   37
5   Language and knowledge   59
6   Language and communication   85
7   Knowledge, speech and action: the halfway mark   99
8   Problem-solving   103
9   Learning, acting and speaking   127
10 Implications for teaching   144
11 Knowing and doing: what's it all about?   156
    Suggestions for further reading   164
    References and name index   167
    Subject index   175

My grateful thanks to Pat Vasiliou
for all the work she has put into
typing the many drafts of this book.

1

Introduction

There is a special difficulty about trying to write a book about memory, thinking and language, since these are just the processes which have gone into writing it. (At least one hopes some memory and thinking have gone into it and it is certainly presented in written language.) The equivalent volume to this in the earlier Essential Psychology series had the title *Thinking and Language*. The implication was that thinking and language could be treated as independent psychological activities. Interestingly there were many scattered references to the influence of memory on thought and language. Ten years on, the role of knowledge stored in memory has moved to the centre of the stage. Mental representations of knowledge based on past experiences, and the mental processes which exploit knowledge in order to interpret and act in the world, are seen as central issues in psychology.

This concern with representations and processes is a trademark of cognitive psychology. Over the past thirty years cognitive psychology has emerged as an identifiable theoretical standpoint for explaining human behaviour. There have been many attempts to define cognitive psychology as a distinctive branch of psychology, comparable with social psychology, physiological psychology and abnormal psychology. Potentially the cognitive approach can be applied to any area of human activity. Children's development can be charted in terms of acquiring more and more complex mental representations, as implied in the work of Piaget. Social interactions depend on the way people represent the intentions and actions of other people. Perceiving the world through our senses results in mental representations of the environment. Indeed it has been claimed (Mandler, 1985) that cognitive psychology 'is well on its way to becoming mainstream psychology'.

Opposed to this is a much narrower definition of cognitive psychology as being concerned with cognition. Cognition is defined in the *Shorter Oxford Dictionary* as 'The action or faculty of knowing; knowledge, consciousness, a product of such an action'; in other words, knowing and being consciously aware. This limits the topic of cognitive psychology to conscious knowledge and those features of the environment we are aware of. In my own environment I am conscious of thinking what to say, writing these words, Handel playing on the radio, someone hammering outside, my unfinished coffee and the names of some people I am planning to ring up later. But there are many other aspects of my behaviour of which I am completely unaware, for instance the movements of the pen with which I wrote the individual letters on this page. A further contrast is between 'cold' rational cognition and two other 'hot' aspects of the mind: conation – which refers to the will – and emotion. Of course, in the real world which humans inhabit, reasoning is often coloured by emotion and thinking serves ulterior purposes. Nevertheless, cognitive psychologists have sometimes been described as being interested only in people as 'disembodied heads'.

The area of psychology covered in this book is not as wide as the empire-building definition of cognitive psychology; nor is it concerned solely with conscious cognition. Because of this ambiguity about the realm of cognitive psychology, I have preferred to retain for the title of this book the more traditional terms: memory, thinking and language. Another reason for my choice of title is that my treatment differs in emphasis from most of the never-ending stream of books on cognitive psychology. It is a generally accepted view that cognitive psychology should be equated with an information processing model of human functioning. In this context information processing is defined as the processing of symbols which represent information. The significance of symbols is that they 'stand for' external events. Mental representations of knowledge are symbolic representations of the world. Processes like thinking, knowing and acting depend on manipulating internally represented symbols. But the information processing approach carries with it other connotations besides this neutral definition of symbol processing. Since the 1950s the guiding metaphor for developing theories of cognition has been the brain as a computer, an analogy which has had a profound effect on the development of cognitive psychology. The brain is thought of as a computer with input and output facilities and a program of instructions for carrying out operations on the data stored in its memory database. A crucial feature of computers is that they, too, are information processing systems. In human terms this means that information from the environment has to be internally represented so that various mental computations can be carried out. Traditionally information processing theories have been formulated as 'box and arrow' models in which information flows through a series of processing stages. The model in Figure 1 is a typical example of a psychological theory which implies that information input from the environment is encoded into different types of symbols as it is passed from one store to another.

This notion of memory stores has had an enormous influence on models of cognition. In textbooks on cognitive psychology theories are usually presented in the order of the stores shown in the 'multi-store' model in Figure 1, beginning with theories of perception, moving on to theories of short-term memory and

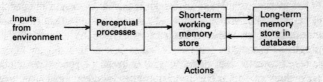

Figure 1 Information processing 'multi-store' model.

finally to theories of long-term memory. I have preferred to take as my starting-point the central role of knowledge representations in long-term memory, working outwards to demonstrate their influence on interpretations of inputs and on the planning and execution of actions. While everyone acknowledges the importance of interactions between knowledge and input information, there is a tendency to look at each stage in isolation. My aim in starting with knowledge is to draw attention to central issues concerning the selection of relevant information and actions to achieve perceived needs. Formulating questions like this emphasizes the integrated nature of cognitive activities, which is reflected in the three major themes listed below.

1 The central role of knowledge in interpreting the environment.
2 The processes by which knowledge gets translated into speech and action.
3 The principles underlying the learning of facts and acts, strategies and procedures for action.

In fact a possible title for this book could have been *Knowledge, Action and Learning*, to emphasize that knowledge informs all thinking, learning, speech and action.

The intertwined nature of human cognitive activities has certainly not made the planning of this book an easy task. The first difficulty is how to parcel out topics under neat chapter headings. A further problem is that, despite the formal distinction between scientific theories and the experiments designed to test them, psychological theories of memory, thinking and language often stem from preconceived ideas about human capabilities. If a psychologist believes that there is no essential difference between human thought and the way a rat learns to run down a maze, then he or she will be likely to design experiments in which human beings are hard put to display anything but rat-like behaviour. On the other hand, a belief in the complexity of human mental processes encourages experiments in which people are given the opportunity to solve complicated problems requiring goal-directed reasoning and creative thinking.

My principle has been to group areas of research together according to the theories and methodologies most commonly used to investigate memory, thinking and language. As will

4

become all too clear, there is no single theoretical framework capable of explaining all human thought and action. However, in the final two chapters, I have attempted my own synthesis of some implications of cognitive psychology for learning and teaching. A linking theme throughout is to characterize the knowledge and problem-solving strategies of those recognized as experts and to identify procedures which may succeed in transforming novices into experts.

Clearly in a book of this size it is impossible to cover all the psychological research which has been done on memory, thinking and language. Rather than attempting to sample the full range of evidence, I have preferred to concentrate on a representative selection of experiments, describing them in sufficient detail to get over the flavour of cognitive research. This has inevitably meant that some very important areas have been mentioned only in passing, for instance cognitive development, individual differences, nonverbal communication, theories of word recognition and models of reading (but see other volumes in the New Essential Psychology series: Turner, 1984; Shackleton and Fletcher, 1984; Gahagan, 1984; Barber, 1987).

2

Thinking and knowledge

It may seem obvious to the layman that thinking, knowledge and intelligence are interconnected. Indeed, they are often defined in terms of each other, intelligence being defined as knowing how to think constructively. Yet, almost from the first emergence of psychology as a subject for study, there has been a division between psychometricians, whose aim is to devise tests of intelligent thinking, and experimental psychologists who study the general characteristics of human thinking and knowledge. I shall be referring to both these traditions and their implications for theories designed to explain intelligent behaviour.

What is thinking?

If asked to define thinking, most people would probably agree on a list of mental activities, including some of the following: day-dreams, wishes, having ideas, philosophical theorizing, making decisions, planning a holiday, working out a problem. How do we arrive at such a list? Essentially by scanning the thoughts which pass through our conscious minds. Clearly there is some quality which enables us to distinguish between the mental activity we call thinking and other more physically overt kinds of behaviour. For one thing, thinking seems to be private and internal to ourselves, in the sense that we are free to conjure up the world – and try out various courses of action in our minds without necessarily telling other people what we are thinking or committing ourselves to action. It has been argued that it is this property of being able to run through actions symbolically rather than in actuality that constitutes human thinking, in the same way that a bridge-builder will create models to try out stresses and strains without going to the expense of building a full-scale bridge. Yet, if we are totally honest, perhaps the most conspicuous quality of moment-to-moment thinking is its fragmentary nature, attention flitting around from topic to topic. It sometimes seems as if our minds are a stage and that we have no control over the entries and exits of random thoughts, images and conjectures.

Despite this everyday experience, most definitions of intelligence stress sheer 'brain power', meaning the ability to think things through in a logical way and to adapt thinking to the problem in hand. Within the psychometric tradition of intelligence testing, the aim has been to measure 'pure' intelligence, as demonstrated by the ability to reason and to follow a consistent train of logical deductions. In conventional IQ tests, tasks are selected which (a) have one right answer and (b) produce large differences in scores to discriminate between individuals with supposedly different levels of intelligence. A full account of the development of IQ tests is given in another book in this series (Shackleton and Fletcher, 1984).

Insight and creativity

Emphasis on the reasoning required to solve well-defined logical problems masks another aspect of human thinking. This is the ability to tackle novel and open-ended problems. One well-known example is the nine dot problem. The task is to draw four straight lines (without raising your pencil from the paper) which will pass through all nine dots.

If you try this for yourself you may find that, like most people, you have represented the problem to yourself as having to draw straight lines which keep within the boundaries of the square. But this particular problem can be solved only by taking an imaginative leap which allows you to draw lines that go outside the square (see solution in Figure 3 at the end of this chapter). The sudden reformulation of a problem which makes a solution obvious is often called insight.

During the 1920s and 1930s the Gestalt group of psychologists, Kohler, Koffka and Wertheimer, argued strongly that thinking depends on the overall structure of the perceptual field. The problems worked on by the Gestalt psychologists tended to have a strong perceptual bias, such as the classic experiments by Kohler, in which he claimed that apes could show insight into the perceptual relations necessary to use one stick to reach another longer stick in order to reach a banana. In a case like this it is easy to see how Gestalt laws about restructuring the perceptual field could affect the way a problem-solver gains 'insight' – a perceptual metaphor – into a possible solution. It is more difficult to see how one would specify the perceptual factors involved in solving a purely abstract logical problem for which there is no perceptual representation (yet notice my unconscious use of the metaphor 'see' in this sentence). Psychologists working in the Gestalt tradition have used a wide variety of problems, ranging from those most clearly dependent on perceptual restructuring, for example Katona's (1940) matchstick problems, to abstract problems which require a grasp of underlying principles. What they all have in common is that they are complex rather than simple and that their solutions are by no means obvious. A famous example is Duncker's (1945) classic radiation problem: 'Given a human being with an

8

inoperable stomach tumour, and rays which destroy organic tissue at sufficient intensity, by what procedure can one free him of the tumour by these rays and at the same time avoid destroying the healthy tissue which surrounds it?' Duncker was one of the first experimenters to use the method of getting the people taking parts as subjects in his experiment to talk aloud while trying to solve the problem, producing what are now called verbal protocols.

Duncker analysed the various suggestions made by his subjects as attempts to solve the main goal by setting up subgoals, for example avoiding contact between the rays and healthy tissue, desensitizing or immunizing the healthy tissue, reducing the intensity of the rays on the way. The point Duncker is making is that these proposals are not just trial and error stabs at solving the problem but are geared to a prior analysis of functional types of solution. The proposed methods result from a reformulation of the overall structure of the problem, from which certain kinds of solutions naturally follow. A breakdown of the suggestions made by one of Duncker's most creative solvers is shown in Figure 2.

In case you are wondering, Duncker's preferred solution was to disperse the rays by sending a lot of weak rays from different directions so that they would meet in sufficient intensity at the tumour. Certainly this 'dispersion' solution requires 'insight'; but reading records of his subjects' thinking aloud protocols, one gets the distinct impression that Duncker as experimenter was rejecting certain suggestions and leading his subjects by hints to a more appropriate solution. The whole thrust of the Gestalt tradition was to help people to restructure a perceptual problem space so as to achieve a novel although, of course, also an appropriate solution. The Gestalt psychologists were more interested in the general principles underlying creative problem-solving than in the question of why some subjects produced several solutions, while other subjects never solved Duncker's problem despite all the hints they were given.

In contrast, the whole issue about what makes some people more creative than others attracted a lot of attention in the early 1960s in the wake of American worries about the USSR winning the race to put up the first sputnik into space. Guilford (1959), in a comprehensive analysis of the components of intelligence,

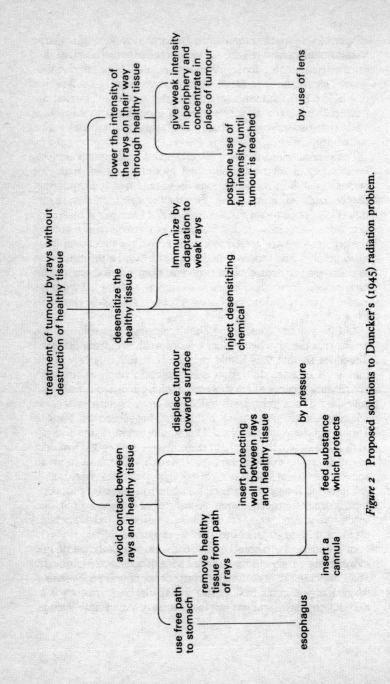

Figure 2 Proposed solutions to Duncker's (1945) radiation problem.

included tests of convergent thinking and divergent thinking. Typical tests of divergent thinking are thinking of all possible uses of a brick or producing as many consequences as possible which might follow from a situation in which everyone suddenly became blind. It should be noted that Guilford implicitly assumed that people would produce relevant rather than truly anarchic responses. Getzels and Jackson (1963) equated high scores on divergence tests with 'creativity' in order to compare 'High Creative' children and 'High IQ' children with reference to school performance and other measures. Despite later criticisms of Getzels and Jackson's attempt to distinguish between intelligence and creativity as two separate abilities, their study gave rise to extensive research identifying different cognitive styles, for example divergers/convergers (Hudson, 1968), impulsiveness/reflectivity (Baron, 1985), 'conservative' assimilation of new experiences as opposed to 'liberal' accommodation of old strategies (Horn, 1986), holists and serialists (Pask, 1976).

Thinking and knowledge

The approaches to thinking and intelligence discussed so far assume that there is such a thing as general thinking and creative abilities which people can apply across a whole range of problems, regardless of what skills a particular task requires; in other words, that intelligent thinking is 'content free'. As you probably know, IQ tests are specifically designed to be as 'content free' as possible. Any tests that require specific knowledge are suspected of being unfair. The criticism of vocabulary tests, for instance, is that they depend on a person's education rather than being a measure of natural 'brainpower'. This laudable obsession with devising knowledge-free culture-fair tests has propagated the belief that there is such a thing as 'pure' intelligence.

Most psychological theories have been geared to discovering mental processes common to all human thinking. Rather than looking at the reasons why some individuals are better at doing certain problems than others, the aim is to illuminate general problem-solving strategies. A further requirement of both IQ tests and psychological experiments is that the people being investigated are presumed to be naive, coming to a task with no prior experience. In the interests of measuring pure intelligence, practice and hints on how to do IQ tests are frowned on as giving children unfair advantages. To study the general characteristics of human problem-solving, it is considered essential for the people used as subjects in psychological experiments to be beginners. Studies of creativity and insight also encourage novel solutions rather than the use of well-tried procedures. Once subjects have discovered the solution to the Duncker radiation problem or the nine dot problem, they do not easily forget it. From this point of view they became useless as subjects, leading to the need to recruit a constant supply of naive subjects.

In complete contrast to this notion of thinking in a vacuum is another common-sense view that intelligence consists of knowing how to do things. Skilled mechanics who transmit their know-how to an apprentice, the largely unconscious social skills that enable us to adapt to new situations, the successful runner working out a strategy for a race, surely these all count as examples of intelligent behaviour and yet they are heavily dependent on previous knowledge and experience. Rather than being a matter of general intelligence and creativity, performance may depend on a facility for acquiring and exploiting knowledge. Since no one can know everything, one would expect the same person to be capable of expert performance in one area while being a complete novice in another.

At this stage it may be helpful to draw up a list of problem situations according to the amount of prior knowledge and thinking required to deal with them.

Levels of problem-solving

Level 1: Already-known facts (for example that Paris is the capital of France).

Level 2: Precise rules can be learnt for obtaining a solution (for example a formula for doing long division sums).

Level 3: Skills have to be picked up while doing a task (for example using maps or learning to drive).

Level 4: A general method is known but particular responses have to be selected and evaluated (for example doing a crossword puzzle or playing chess).

Level 5: A problem has to be reformulated in order to produce some unusual method of solution (for example inventing a new kind of windscreen wiper or solving the Duncker radiation problem).

Level 6: The problem itself has to be invented (for example Newton realizing that the falling apple needed an explanation).

Looking at these levels of problem-solving, it is obvious that the amount of creative thought required depends on each individual's past experiences with similar problems. A person who has no previous knowledge of long division will be in a totally different position from someone for whom it is a trivial problem. More subtly de Groot (1965) discovered some very interesting differences about the perceptions of chess masters and less experienced players. He talks about a 'treasury of ready experience' which enables the more experienced player to 'see' the position of the chess pieces in configurations which represent possible patterns of alternative moves. Apparently it is impossible for chess masters even to imagine how the board looks to a beginner, who has to work out laboriously the consequences of possible moves. Comparisons between novice and expert chess players (Chase and Simon, 1973) confirmed de Groot's observations that chess masters are much better at recalling and reconstructing patterns of chess pieces on the board than non-experts. This holds only as long as the pieces are in a game position; experts have no advantage over novices at recalling random arrangements of pieces.

If experts can rely on prior knowledge of situations and well-learned procedures, this leaves us with the paradox that it is novices who habitually have to face new problems and discover creative solutions (creative for them at least). Underlying most research into creativity is the assumption that creativity is best, relegating the poor convergers to the dullness of conventional intelligence. Yet if you look back to the six levels of problem-solving, it is more efficient to know that Paris is the capital of France or to be familiar with the rules of long division. It is chess masters who automatically recognize game positions, drawing upon their already acquired knowledge of configurations of chess pieces, while it is less expert players who have to discover new 'creative' solutions each time they play. To take an extreme example, it was extremely creative of Newton to discover gravity, but we can learn the principles of gravity in the absence of the superb creative abilities needed to discover gravity from scratch. Perhaps the best summary of this point of view is to point to the rarity of novel solutions, or even of long bouts of sustained thinking, when tackling problems. It is far more characteristic for humans to try out old ideas than to go through the pain of learning new procedures. Mental laziness is typical in most situations, the only incentive for new learning being the pay-off of becoming an expert and so avoiding the need to think so hard. In general, the more we know, the less we have to think.

Knowledge and action

These last remarks may seem to imply a rather gloomy assessment of the human capacity for innovative thinking. However, reliance on known procedures is a recipe for fast action. Interpretations of events in the environment are inevitably coloured by previous experience. Faced with a dangerous situation, it may be better to run than to stop and think. On some occasions a person's mental representation of a situation will stimulate an immediate action response; at other times, the best response may be to think through several possible actions. Knowledge plays a central role in all this. It affects the way people perceive situations in the first place, which in turn activates previously learned procedures for dealing with the new situation. To complete the circle, the consequences of actions will themselves be stored in the form of new knowledge for deciding about future actions. This allows for the possibility of learning from new experiences, noting procedures which have proved to be effective for dealing with a variety of situations. From this point of view, thinking itself is a well-learned procedure for interpreting inputs, retrieving relevant knowledge and selecting appropriate actions from each individual's repertoire of behaviours.

We are left with the question of where all this knowledge comes from. On the basis of knowledge about a specific topic domain, experts achieve rapid interpretations of the significance of situations, are able to retrieve relevant information from memory and to select an appropriate strategy for any problems that may arise. In contrast, novices are less likely to perceive helpful analogies with previous situations and so have to fall back on more general problem-solving strategies. To take just one example, what we mean by a skilled manager is someone who is sensitive to situations, including other people's intentions and reactions, and has a wide range of potential responses. It is not an easy matter, though, to combine a reliance on learned procedures with the flexibility needed to adapt to novel events. The expert's knowledge facilitates the rapid absorption of information and the production of appropriate responses. The novice may find learning harder but retain a refreshing new outlook on an old set of problems.

Cognitive psychologists have made many brave attempts to model mental representations of knowledge and the processes which enable knowledge to be used in interpreting events, planning actions and acquiring new knowledge. These cognitive models will form the backbone of this book. The interplay between old knowledge and new experience will be a recurring theme.

Conclusions

Four main issues have been raised in this chapter, which in our present state of knowledge must be phrased as questions rather than as answers.

1 Is there such a thing as 'pure' intelligence, which can be exploited in all types of thinking, or does the performance of experts rely mainly on task-specific knowledge, thus cutting down the need for mental effort?

2 How can the creativity and insight required for solving problems be reconciled with people's reliance on already acquired procedures?

3 What is the relation between acquired knowledge, interpretations of new experiences, actions and their consequences, and the learning of new knowledge?

4 Are there any essential differences between the way experts deal with familiar situations as compared to the approach of a novice coming new to the task?

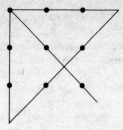

Figure 3 A solution to the nine dot problem.

3

The structure of knowledge

If there is one feature that distinguishes the emergence of cognitive psychology, it is an emphasis on mental representations of knowledge. The argument goes as follows: if a large proportion of intelligent behaviour is accounted for by already acquired knowledge, that knowledge must be mentally represented in memory. If mental representations are necessary for interpreting objects and events in the external environment, objects and events must be internally represented as symbolic concepts. It is these mental concepts that constitute our knowledge of the world which underpins the planning and execution of actions. From this point of view, the ability to act depends on rapid access to relevant knowledge – having facts at our finger tips rather than stored away in some inaccessible corner of memory.

What is knowledge?

It is tempting to think of knowledge as something very rarified, displayed only by philosophers and scholars. However, as used in psychology, knowledge refers to all the information we have stored in memory, including common-sense knowledge. It can be thought of as a record of past experiences, knowledge of facts and know-how about what to do and when. People are constantly, if mostly unconsciously, relying on remembered experiences to carry them through each day. When I sit down to write this book, I am exploiting my learned ability to write English and my stored knowledge about psychology; mental representations concerned with psychology should come crowding into my mind. Obviously it is the content of these memories which is relevant to the activity of writing about psychology. But my ability to dredge up information about a psychology experiment I vaguely remember depends on links between different items in memory. I may think of the general subject area, browse through the names of psychologists I know about and scientific journals I have read. The point is that retrieving information would be impossible if memories were random. Just as locating a book in a library relies on a well-organized catalogue, so gaining access to an appropriate fact, experience or plan of action depends on the way in which knowledge is structured in memory.

One of the earliest and neatest experiments showing that people rely on structured knowledge was carried out by Katona (1940), a psychologist working in the Gestalt tradition. He presented subjects with the series of digits 581215192226. He then manipulated the way they were likely to structure their memory of those digits by telling one group of subjects to memorize them, a second group to find a rule or principle involved in generating the digits, and a third group that the figure represented government expenditure. On an immediate test there was not much difference between the three groups. But when they were tested again after three weeks, none of the rote learning group could remember the digits, the rule group had a go at producing a sequence (incidentally adding a 3 and 4 alternately to the numbers), while some of the 'expenditure' group remembered 5.8 billion.

During the next two decades, which marked the heyday of verbal learning experiments, subjects had to repeat back lists of nonsense syllables, digits and words in the exact order they heard them. As soon as the revolutionary step was taken of allowing subjects to recall items in any order they wished, these so-called 'free recall' experiments immediately revealed that people group items into categories in order to aid recall. In fact they make use of practically any cue, prior associations between words, sorting items into categories, even alphabetical cues, only in the last resort falling back on passive rehearsal and rote recall. Since lists of words grouped into categories, such as animals, furniture and toys, were found to be much easier to learn than lists of random words, it seems reasonable to assume that mental concepts may be organized in the same way.

Semantic hierarchies

It has proved a very persuasive idea that knowledge representations are organized in memory as a semantic network of interconnected concepts which represent semantic relations between categories of concepts. One influential model was Collins and Quillian's (1969) hierarchical semantic network in which categories like animals and plants are defined as concepts which are related to each other in various ways. As shown in Figure 4, the links between the concepts represent relations between categories. Thus the concept 'canary' is a member of the 'bird' category. In addition concepts are defined in terms of defining features, for example a canary 'can sing' and 'is yellow'. Birds have features like 'has wings', 'can fly', 'has feathers'.

Quillian's theory was designed to be implemented as a computer program which could comprehend sentences on the basis of the information about concepts in its database. This program, known as the Teachable Language Comprehender (TLC), was an early attempt to model human conceptual knowledge, a prototype of later knowledge-based computer systems. Let us suppose the model is faced with a sentence like *A canary is a bird*. In order to understand this sentence, it is necessary to search through the semantic hierarchy in the database to retrieve information about the concepts 'canary' and 'bird'. Given a sentence like *A canary is a bird*, a search is activated throughout the hierarchy starting from both the 'canary' and 'bird' concepts until the two searches intersect to provide a link between the two concepts. The longer it takes for a

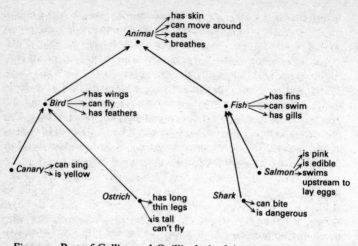

Figure 4 Part of Collins and Quillian's (1969) semantic hierarchy for animals.

path to be found to where the two concepts interact, the longer the response. Thus in Figure 4 there is a direct link between 'canary' and 'bird'. However, the sentence *A canary is an animal* would require a search further up the hierarchy to connect the concepts 'canary' and 'animal'. The same principle applies to sentences about features. *A canary can sing* refers to a direct link between 'canary' and 'can sing'. But to understand the sentence *A canary breathes* a path would need to be activated up the hierarchy to the 'animal' concept in order to retrieve the facts that a canary is a bird, a bird is an animal, animals breathe and therefore a canary can breathe.

You may well be wondering what all this has got to do with human memory. In the introductory chapter I referred to the computer analogy of human functioning. The basic idea is that the knowledge stored in human memory is like the information stored in the database of a computer. So the implication of the Collins and Quillian model is that people's knowledge of objects in the environment is organized as a semantic hierarchy of concepts and categories. Of course, the network in Figure 4 displays only a tiny fraction of all human knowledge. It is meant to reflect biological knowledge that cats and dogs and birds are animals, that pigs can't fly, that elephants have trunks and that whales are mammals. To represent the vast amount of knowledge in human memory there would have to be thousands, perhaps millions, of other concept hierarchies, for example about man-made objects, abstract ideas, and many others. In addition there are many links between hierarchies, for example canaries are often kept in man-made cages. One reason why Quillian's biological hierarchy was taken up by psychologists was that his model was experimentally tested by Collins and Quillian (1969) using a sentence verification task. Subjects were asked to judge (verify) whether sentences are true or false, for example *A canary is a bird, A shark is a bird, A canary can sing, A canary can breathe*. The prediction was that people would take longer to decide about sentences which involve longer searches through the network. The results of the experiment confirmed this prediction. Sentences which require a search to be made over more links do indeed take longer to verify than sentences like *A canary can sing* and *A canary is a bird* which exploit direct links between concepts. Thus subjects responded faster to sentences like *A canary can sing* and *A canary is a bird* and took longer to verify sentences like *A canary can breathe* and *A canary is an animal*. Times for responses to false sentences like *A shark is a bird* are more difficult to explain since it is not clear at what point a search would be abandoned. At a high enough level in a semantic network, all paths intersect. Sharks and birds are both animals and yet they have to be differentiated at the lower level representing the distinction between birds and fish.

In view of the extra time taken to retrieve information from indirect links higher up the hierarchy, one might question whether it would not be more efficient to store all the information about canaries with the concept 'canary'. If all the defining features of canaries, 'can sing', 'is yellow', 'can fly', 'breathes', were listed at the 'canary' level, then all sentences about canaries could be quickly 'read off' from direct links. There is, however, a significant disadvantage. Features like 'breathes' and 'exists' would have to be stored many many times over, with every example of organisms which breathe, and entities which exist. Even in the simple little network shown in Figure 4, the features 'breathes' and 'has skin' would have to be stated for every concept individually. Canaries breathe and have skin, but so do ostriches and sharks, birds and fish. So it is in the interests of cognitive economy that features are stored once only at the highest level in the hierarchy to which they apply.

This model for retrieving information from memory is known as 'inheritance', because each concept in the hierarchy 'inherits' features from higher level concepts. A canary inherits the 'breathes' feature from the 'animal' node and the 'has wings' feature from the 'bird' node. Another way of putting this is as follows: if it is known that a canary is a bird, it is possible to *infer* that it must have wings and feathers and can fly. One assumption of this type of model is that it is more economical to carry out searches up the network in order to infer features like 'breathes' rather than to store them with the individual concepts where they can be directly looked up, for example 'a canary can breathe'. If the brain is like a computer, this would be tantamount to saying that it is quicker to compute inheritance relations rather than to look up items directly.

Another point to notice about the Collins and Quillian network is the contrast between the defining features of high-level concepts like 'birds' and 'animals' and the more specialized features of particular birds and animals. At the higher levels it is possible to indicate defining features of animals and birds. All animals have skin and breathe. All birds can fly. Concepts at lower levels in the network are only allocated more idiosyncratic features, the fact that a canary is yellow or an ostrich can't fly. Unfortunately this ducks the exceptionally tricky issue of how to reconcile the general characteristics of all birds with the special characteristics of particular types of birds. It is not so bad when a particular bird has an *extra* feature like canaries being able to sing especially good songs, which can be added on to general bird-like features. But what about ostriches which actually contradict the 'flying' characteristics of birds? How is it possible to *stop* the inference that ostriches are birds and so 'can fly'? The memory system would have to be given a rule like 'check out all the features of a low-level concept and make inferences only if there is no contradictory feature'. In other words, first check that ostriches can't fly *before* making an inference that all birds can fly. This obviously adds a lot of complexity to what seemed a nice and simple hierarchy. Yet another problem is how to deal with features like 'large' which are true of some birds and fishes but not of others. It would be misleading to include a 'size' defining feature for the animal category. Birds and fishes are normally quite small, compared with other animals like horses and elephants. But ostriches are 'big' for a bird. A 'rat' may be 'big' for a rodent, but 'small' in the context of the whole animal category. My pet dog Fido may be so small that he fits into no obvious dog category; in fact if he is yellow and can sing, he might even be mistaken for a canary!

Feature comparison models

Theories which have addressed the question of how objects are recognized as belonging to one category rather than another have had to face the issue of how an ostrich can be categorized as a bird even though it can't fly and so lacks one of the most important defining features of the bird category. In an attempt to get round this problem, some theories have reverted to the idea of storing a list of all the features of a concept directly with that concept. Thus the concept 'canary' is represented as a list of all the defining features of a canary, that it is a bird, that it is an animal, that it is a physical object, that it has feathers, can breathe, is yellow and sings, plus any characteristic features, like being kept as a pet in a cage, which are not necessarily true of all canaries. The concept 'pig' would have animal-like features as well as characteristic features like being a farmyard animal. The concept 'bird' would be represented by a set of defining features and characteristic features which would include all the bird-like features, can fly, and so on, all the animal and physical object features, and also characteristic features, for example 'fairly small'. Higher-level concepts like 'animal' and 'physical object' would be defined by appropriate features, although there might be fewer characteristic features which would be true of all animals and physical objects.

It should be obvious from all this that features would have to be repeated many times. Very general features like 'exists' and 'has substance' would be attached to all concepts which are physical objects, including tables and chairs, as well as animals and birds. The feature 'grows' is true of most living things, 'can breathe' of all animals including humans, 'can fly' has to be attached to all birds except ostriches, emus and penguins. While this system may seem to flout the principles of cognitive economy, it might perform better as an object recognition device. Recognizing a canary as a bird would involve comparing all the features of canaries and all the features of birds to test whether there is enough overlap of features to justify the identification. Canaries and birds share a very large number of general features, for example 'exists', 'grows', 'breathes', as well as bird-like features, for example 'can fly', 'has feathers'. The extra 'can sing' and 'is yellow' features of a canary would be outweighed by the similarity of all the other features. One big advantage of this system is that it allows for the possibility of comparing both defining features and idiosyncratic features. For instance deciding whether an ostrich is a bird would involve a comparison between the features which birds and ostriches share in common, like 'feathers' and 'beaks' as well as features which are different, like 'large' as opposed to 'probably small' and 'fly' versus 'can't fly'. The question then is, how many features do concepts have to have in common to be judged as being a member of a category?

A typical example of a feature comparison theory is that of Smith, Shoben and Rips (1974). According to their model, sentences like *A canary is a bird* are judged by comparing the defining and characteristic features for the concepts 'canary' and 'bird' to see if they match. The Smith, Shoben and Rips model built in a match criterion so that a lot of overlap between the features of two concepts will result in a fast initial response of 'yes', for example *A robin is a bird*. Little overlap of common features will result in a fast 'no' response, for example *A fish is a stone*. A medium amount of overlap, for example *A shark is a bird*, will take longer to reject or accept because sharks and birds share a lot of the same features such as breathing, being animals, having skin, can swim, eating, may be eaten, and so on. For in-between cases of this kind, there is a second comparison stage, in which only defining features are considered. Although both sharks and birds are animals, a special defining feature of sharks is 'has gills' while a defining feature of birds is 'can fly'. Of course, this rather begs the question of deciding which are the most appropriate defining features for differentiating concepts; why are 'has gills' and 'can fly' more relevant than a shared feature like 'breathes'? Nevertheless, experiments have confirmed that subjects do take less time to reject obviously different concepts like stones and trees than concepts which share more potential features like sharks and birds, pigs and trees (Collins and Quillian, 1970).

It may seem rather unlikely that people compare whole sets of features every time they recognize an object, although the fact that we are not conscious of complex comparison processes does not, of course, mean that they do not occur. However, feature comparison models fall at the same hurdles as the Collins and Quillian semantic hierarchy network. How is a decision made about the amount of overlap in features required to identify a category? What happens when an object has untypical or contradictory features? If an ostrich does not have the defining 'can fly' bird feature, it should be ruled out as a bird at the stage when defining features are compared. On the other hand, a whale might share so many defining and characteristic features with the fish category that it is recognized as a fish at the initial comparison stage. Despite their uncharacteristically large size, ostriches have quite a lot of the defining features of birds, but lack the one important defining feature of flying. Whales, despite their uncharacteristically large size, share many defining features with fishes, like swimming underwater, but share other 'non-fishy' defining features with mammals, like suckling their young. The unresolved issue is what weight should be given to defining features and characteristic features in decisions about objects. Collins and Loftus (1975) make the additional point that knowledge that whales are mammals and that a sponge is an animal is usually based on the fact that people have been told about these categories; in fact they often don't know which are the relevant features to compare, as would be required by a feature comparison model. Collins and Loftus argue for a hybrid model in which some typical features of concepts are stored with each concept but more abstract and esoteric features are retrieved by inferring knowledge about animals, or perhaps by recalling special information about oddball categories like whales and sponges.

Typicality and prototypes

One main problem for both semantic hierarchies and feature-based models is that they depend on the feasibility of identifying the defining features of categories. It is assumed that there are lists of features which define canaries, poodles, dogs, birds, fish, plants, animals and living things. It is not, however, anything like as easy as it sounds to list all the defining features of a concept. There are formal concepts for which all the defining features can be listed, for example the properties which define a triangle or a prime number. It may be possible, too, to list defining features for 'abstract' high-level biological concepts like 'animal'. But when it comes to different species of dogs and birds, what counts as a defining feature? There are some birds which cannot fly and some dogs with no tails; canaries that refuse to sing and dogs that don't bark. The problem becomes even more acute for man-made objects like furniture. There are one-legged tables and chairs with no legs at all. From facts like these, it seems that many categories cannot be defined conclusively by a set of defining features.

A further assumption of category models is that all examples of a category are usually assumed to be equal. A canary is a bird and an ostrich is a bird just as much as a robin is a bird. Cats and whales are both defined as mammals. In Figure 4 there are single links between 'ostrich' and 'bird' and between 'canary' and 'bird'. Yet most people would agree that a canary is a more 'typical' bird than an ostrich. Many experiments have confirmed this intuition by demonstrating that subjects agree among themselves about typical and untypical instances of categories (Rosch, 1975; Smith, Shoben and Rips 1974) and that reaction times are faster to statements about typical examples of categories than statements about less typical examples.

Various theories have attempted to deal with these typicality effects. Collins and Loftus (1975) extended Collins and Quillian's hierarchical search model by suggesting that it takes less time for activation to spread along well-used 'typical' links. Thus the link between 'canary' and 'bird' will be activated quicker than the between 'ostrich' and 'bird', resulting in a faster response to *A canary is a bird*. Feature comparison theories accounted for typicality effects on the basis that robins and canaries share more characteristic features with the bird category than do ostriches and penguins. Consequently the greater overlap of features between canaries and birds will lead to a quicker response. These proposals can be thought of as 'patches' to salvage theories which essentially depend on the notion that concepts are represented in terms of identifiable defining features.

However, Rosch (1975, 1978) took the very different tack of proposing that concepts are not represented by defining features which clearly differentiate one concept from another. Drawing on evidence about people's reactions to typical categories, she suggested that concepts are stored as prototype representations of typical birds, typical pieces of furniture, and so on. When subjects were asked to name typical instances of categories, they showed remarkable unanimity that robins are typical birds and that tables and chairs are typical examples of furniture, in a way that ostriches, pianos and wastepaper baskets are not. The 'bird' prototype can be thought of as a composite category which reflects typical bird-like features. Prototypes are abstract concepts in the sense that no particular bird may be quite a perfect example of the essence of birdiness. However, some birds are nearer the prototype than others. This would explain why it takes less time to respond to typical birds like *A robin is a bird* than to atypical birds like *A penguin is a bird*.

One consequence of Rosch's rejection of defining features is that the less typical examples of a category may share some features with a neighbouring concept. Although typical tables may have four legs and a top, the boundaries of the 'table' concept is wide enough to allow for a three-legged table. But stools also have three legs and so do some chairs. This means that the boundaries between the 'table', 'chair' and 'stool' concepts are 'fuzzy' in the sense that they may share features, for instance tables, chairs and stools can all have three legs. To decide whether an object is a table or a stool cannot be definitely decided on the basis of the defining feature of having three or four legs. This fuzziness is undoubtedly an appealing characteristic of Rosch's theory. However, the appeal to fuzzy concepts does not of itself solve the question of how untypical concepts are recognized. For Rosch to say that ostriches are untypical birds and that whales are untypical mammals begs the question of how we know that ostriches and penguins *are* birds, typical or otherwise. For people who know that whales are mammals, no matter how fuzzy the boundary between mammals and fishes, whales will be classified as untypical mammals rather than as untypical fish.

A rather different aspect of Rosch's theory is her demonstration that certain levels in a semantic hierarchy are more basic than others, representing what she calls basic-level categories. It is more natural to identify an object as a 'table' or as a 'dog' rather than as a 'piece of furniture', an 'animal', a 'kitchen table' or a 'collie'. Rosch explains these basic-level categories as being due to the fact that instances of high-level categories, such as 'birds' and 'furniture', share too few common features. What features do cushions and pianos have in common as pieces of furniture, wrens and ostriches in common as both being birds? In contrast, categories at the lowest levels share too many features to be easily distinguished, for example kitchen chairs are too similar to dining chairs, as are barn owls and tawny owls. Rosch and her colleagues (Rosch *et al.*, 1976) have carried out experiments showing that people produce most features for basic-level categories like 'chair' and 'bird', less for superordinate categories like 'furniture' and 'animal', while for subordinate categories like 'kitchen chair' or 'sparrow' few extra attributes are suggested other than those already given for 'chair' or 'bird' (see Figure 5). Notice that in Figure 5 Rosch had predicted that the names of particular birds like 'sparrow' would be the basic-level category. But from subjects' responses, it is obvious that it is the level of species like birds and dogs that are natural basic-level categories.

Rosch's explanation was that top-level categories do not have sufficient shared features in common to group them together as a single category, while lower-level categories do not have enough separate features to distinguish them from the basic level category. So it is the intermediate-level categories like chairs and tables, birds and dogs, which are easiest to distinguish as identifiable categories. Choice of basic-level categories is, however, relative depending on expertise and the purpose of description. An interior designer may be aware of many subtle features which distinguish different types of chairs; a zoologist may know many biological features which make 'animal' a

Level	Category	Attributes	Category	Attributes
Super ordinate	furniture	none	bird	feathers, head, wings, claws, beak, lays eggs, legs, feet, nests, eyes, flies, tail, chirps, eats flies and worms
Intermediate (predicted basic level)	chair	legs seat back arms comfortable four legs wood holds people – you sit on it	sparrow	as for 'bird' small brown
Subordinate	living-room chair	as for 'chair' plus: large soft cushion	song sparrow	as for 'sparrow'
	kitchen chair	as for 'chair'	field sparrow	as for 'sparrow'

Figure 5 Basic levels.
Source: Rosch *et al.* (1976).

meaningful category. In the context of seeing several dogs in a park, it may be reasonable to refer to a collie in order to distinguish it from all the other dogs. Olson (1970) proposed that people need to mention only things which distinguish one object from another.

Rosch's theory of basic levels has been supported by the observation that if someone says *That's a dog*, people do not take this as referring to disparate aspects of the environment, say a combination of the tail of the dog with the trunk of a tree behind the dog. Moreover, children normally have pointed out to them the names for easily identified categories like 'that's a dog'; 'that's a table' rather than 'that's a piece of furniture', or 'that's an animal' or 'that's a kitchen chair'. It is probable, too, that names are given which refer to prototypical instances, at least in the first place. A child might get confused if told that an ostrich is a bird before being exposed to more typical birds like robins and swallows. Rosch (1973) found that children's responses to typical examples of concepts were much faster than their responses to less typical examples; adults did not show as great a difference. It has also been noted that children often over-generalize concepts, needing to be told that the furry animal over there is not a dog and that the kind gentleman is not 'daddy'. It is interesting to note that children seem to proceed from an initial identification of typical objects to a gradual learning of the features which precisely define different categories of objects. This is, of course, the exact opposite of feature comparison models, which explain identification of objects in terms of comparing already-known defining features.

Basically Rosch's model is a hybrid in which categories are arranged in a semantic hierarchy, the difference being that some levels are considered to be more basic than others. Concepts at each level are defined by overlapping sets of more or less typical features. It should be noted, by the way, that the subjects in Rosch's experiments obviously took her instructions to mean that they should list typical perceptual features of categories, rather than the more abstract features which all animals share, like being animate, or that furniture is typically found in buildings. In another experiment (Armstrong, Gleitman and Gleitman, 1983) subjects were even prepared to say that some digits are more typical of odd numbers than others – for instance, the number 3 was rated as a more typical odd number than 23.

Evaluation of conceptual models

Within psychology, hierarchical networks, list of defining and typical features and prototypes have been thought of as rival models of how concepts are stored in human memory. However, it seems likely that our minds are much more untidy than any of these models, allowing us sometimes to exploit the cognitive economy of hierarchies of biological categories; sometimes to identify the defining attributes of mathematical and scientific concepts; sometimes to trade on similarities between features; other times to use everyday knowledge about typical dogs and what tables are used for. As Roth (1986) pointed out, the very same object can be classified differently, depending on the circumstances, a dog as my pet Fido or as a member of the canine species.

However, a word of warning. Despite the optimistic tone of the last paragraph, there are several so far quite unresolved issues. It simply begs the question to say that humans are capable of multiple categorizations of objects, as and when required. Is a standard lamp infinitely classifiable as an untypical example of furniture, a piece of electrical equipment, a fire risk, a weapon, a work of art, and so on? It is ironic, perhaps, that one of the most common tests of creativity is to ask people to list as many uses as they can think of for objects like bricks and standard lamps. Another dilemma for all category-based models is that identification of an object as a dog or a cup seems to rely on knowledge of general categories; yet each object we encounter is an individual example. It is not often, after all, that we have to verify in the abstract whether *All elephants are mammals* or *A shark is a bird*, or are asked to list the attributes of all tables, or all apples. What people need to know is the best way of dealing with individual elephants, whether they are encountered in a zoo, or charging around on a safari. It is difficult enough to decide whether all poodles are dogs. But what about the even more idiosyncratic features of individual objects, like my pet dog Fido, who is yellow, has no tail, and can sing?

In the course of daily life, one may come across a one-legged chair; most standard lamps also have one leg. Yet it is really unlikely that people confuse chairs and lamps. More important than the perceptual features, so popular with psychologists, are the functions of objects. Tables are for eating off and writing on, lamps are for lighting. A tree stump can be categorized as a picnic table and stars are metaphorical lamps. Dogs and alligators can be pets as well as animals. Tomatoes *are* vegetables when included in a stew however much biologists tell us they should be categorized as fruit. In fact the most characteristic feature of categorization models is that they operate in a vacuum rather than taking into account the situation in which new objects are encountered. It is as if there is an immutable hierarchy which classifies objects into sets of categories once and for all. For most purposes we may think of robins and pigeons as typical birds but we can also respond to pheasants and pigeons as game to be eaten – or protected species depending on one's point of view. How we categorize an object depends crucially on the context in which we encounter it and its relevance to the matter in hand. Labov (1973) gave different instructions to subjects to imagine that they were drinking coffee, drinking soup or arranging flowers. The effect was that the very same object might be categorized as a cup, a bowl or a vase depending on what subjects had been told (see Figure 6). Rather than relying on 'academic' knowledge about hierarchies of concepts and the defining features of categories, humans are constantly experiencing objects in different situational contexts.

Figure 6 Some cups and bowls.
Source: Labov (1973).

Integrating general knowledge about categories of objects with personal experiences of individual objects may be no problem for humans. But it is a very great problem for psychologists attempting to model the way in which general knowledge about concepts interacts with knowledge about the objects and events we encounter from day to day. This distinction between general knowledge and personal experience has become an important issue in cognitive psychology under the guise of semantic memory and episodic memory.

Semantic memory and episodic memory

Tulving (1972) proposed a division of memory into semantic memory and episodic memory. Semantic memory is defined as general knowledge about concepts which has been abstracted from individual experiences. No one remembers the actual time and place when they learned that $2 + 2 = 4$, that *dog* is the name for a member of the canine species, that ostriches are birds which can't fly or that whales are mammals. I can't even pinpoint the first occasion on which I read Tulving's description of semantic and episodic memory. In contrast, episodic memories specify a definite time and place located in our own personal histories. These include both autobiographical events in our past lives and also recent and current episodes, which may eventually be forgotten but are present to us now. Examples of episodes would be the first day I went to school or the telephone call I have just made to the publisher of this book saying it will be with her in the next two weeks.

In some ways it is a pity that Tulving used the terms semantic *memory* and episodic *memory*, which makes it sound as if there are two separate memory stores in the brain. What he was really trying to distinguish is two types of *knowledge*. Some knowledge, although it must originally have come from some definite episode when we were told something, read it in a book or noticed some aspect of the environment, by now has become 'free floating' from its original happening. The models of conceptual knowledge I have discussed in this chapter constitute semantic knowledge of this kind. Other knowledge is based on experiences which we can remember as having happened to ourselves. For a child each encounter with a dog may still be a separate episode. It is not until dogs in general are recognized as belonging to the dog category that we would say that the child understands the concept 'dog'. The semantic concept 'dog' has been abstracted from doggy episodes so that new episodes involving dogs can be related to that concept.

One point that has bedevilled attempts to differentiate semantic and episodic knowledge is the amount of overlap between the two types of knowledge. Examples at each extreme are clear cut, for example episodic memories of my first day at school in contrast to semantic knowledge that robins are birds. But a lot of knowledge is a mishmash of personal experiences and general knowledge; for instance my knowledge about Greece is based both on memories of personal visits and general reading. Since all knowledge must have been acquired through personal experiences in the first place, including what we have read and been told, the distinction seems to come down to a matter of how much information about time and place is still tagged to the original episode.

Linton (1982) carried out an autobiographical experiment over a period of six years. At the end of each day she wrote down on cards two events which had happened to her during the day. Examples would be 'I took my daughter to the dentist' and 'I attended a staff committee meeting'. At monthly intervals she drew out two of these cards at random and tried to remember and date the episodes she had written down. She reported that, as events were constantly repeated, separate episodes began to blur together and could no longer be remembered as specific dated episodes. Unusual incidents had more chance of being remembered even after quite long periods, unless they were completely trivial and forgotten altogether – like the nonsense syllables learnt in a psychological experiment! On the other hand, repeated events, although forgotten as individual episodes, gradually merged into general knowledge about what usually happens at committee meetings. In other words, information which had started out as individual remembered episodes eventually contributed to generalized semantic knowledge.

It is, perhaps, the common fate of most experiences to end up as vague general memories. A notable exeption is the vivid personal memory which retains the feel of having happened to ourselves at a particular time and place. Attempts have been made to explain autobiographical memories – or the lack of them – from the days of Freud onwards. Brown and Kulik (1982) claimed that 'flashbulb memories' are triggered by important events. A lot of people can describe exactly what they were doing when they heard about John F. Kennedy's or John Lennon's assassination. While it may be, as Neisser (1982) suggests, that some striking memories are the result of people telling and retelling the events to themselves and to other people, I am sure we all have vivid personal memories which are private to ourselves – although becoming increasingly less private when probed by psychologists interested in personal memories.

Further support for the notion of a distinction between episodic and semantic knowledge is provided by a curious case reported in a television programme presented by Jonathan Miller in 1986. Clive Wearing was a practising musician who, as a result of a rare virus which caused massive brain damage, had in effect lost his memory for events both before and after his illness. While he could still carry on a conversation, conduct music, use the telephone and knew that he was married, everything that had happened to him was completely wiped out. Whenever he

34

saw his wife, he hugged and hugged her – as if just reunited – with no apparent recollection of having seen her ten minutes ago, or indeed every day of his life. It was as if he had retained semantic knowledge which enabled him to get up in the morning, walk and talk, conduct music, and so on. But the loss of all episodic memories from childhood onwards meant that he could not remember having done these things. His complete loss of memory for personal events made him feel that he was dead without any past. He was able to express this feeling yet would forget immediately that he had expressed it and kept saying it over and over again as if for the first time. He gave the impression of being newborn as far as autobiographical personal experiences were concerned, but that he had retained semantic knowledge which made him aware, albeit temporarily, of what he was missing. The question of why his wife felt that his personality was still intact – apart from his recurrent deep distress about his lost past – is a fascinating, and inexplicable, feature of the case.

Clive Wearing remembered some facts such as his name and his love for his wife, which might be considered to be part of his own autobiographical past. However, there is a difference between autobiographical facts like these, which are no longer tagged with specific time and place information, and memories for actual episodes. I certainly cannot remember the specific occasion when I was first told my name. This distinction between autobiographical facts and event-related personal memories is suggested by an experiment carried out by Conway (1987). He showed that autobiographical facts can be cued by semantic information. For instance it was found that giving subjects a general category name like *fruits* would speed up responses to a question about an autobiographical fact like *Are apples your favourite fruit?* in just the same way as it would facilitate answers to a general knowledge question like *Is an orange a fruit?* In contrast, memories for actual events, like eating some particularly delicious oranges, were best cued by 'personal' hints such as 'Your holiday in Italy' (Conway and Bekerian, 1987).

All these examples point to the complexity of human knowledge. First, there is semantic knowledge about general categories and concepts, on the basis of which objects can be recognized and inferences made about probable features.

Second, there are autobiographical facts, our names, our role in society, our personal likes and dislikes. These can be thought of as relatively stable and consistent facts we know about ourselves. Third, there are personal experiences which are remembered as actual episodes in our lives, which may be idiosyncratic one-off events. The point at which all these shade into each other cannot perhaps be strictly pinpointed. What is clear is that semantic knowledge influences interpretations of new episodes, which in turn alter and update the current state of general and auto-biographical knowledge. The question we shall now turn to is how knowledge provides a framework for interpreting new experiences and new inputs from the environment.

Conclusions

The attempt to distinguish between semantic knowledge of concepts and categories, on the one hand, and personal memories based on individual episodes in day-to-day life, on the other, has raised several important questions, to which we will be returning in later chapters.

1 Is general knowledge of concepts best organized as sets of categories in a semantic hierarchy or as lists of defining and characteristic features?

2 What is the relation between prototypical examples of categories and less typical examples which are nevertheless recognized as falling within the boundary of a concept?

3 It is possible to explain how categories of objects are recognized without taking into account the situation in which an object is encountered?

4 How can general semantic knowledge be reconciled with personal experience of objects and episodes? In what way do these two types of knowledge interact?

4

Active memory

The models of memory discussed in the previous chapter were in effect descriptions of passive memory. I am using the term passive memory to refer to all the knowledge which we have locked up in our minds. It is a moot point whether everything we have ever experienced is recorded in memory. Freud, among others, would maintain that everything is stored but some memories are so traumatic that they have been repressed into the unconscious. From the cognitive psychologist's point of view, all that matters is whether knowledge can be retrieved. So, in contrast to the rather static knowledge about categories of objects discussed in the previous chapter, this chapter will concentrate on the active role played by memory in coping with day-to-day experiences. The organization of knowledge will still be of central importance but the emphasis will be on the interaction between knowledge and new inputs. Rather than relegating idiosyncratic examples to the fuzzy boundaries between prototypes, the aim is to explain how new events can be interpreted in the light of old knowledge. General knowledge influences the way we interpret episodes in the first place. In turn, general knowledge is constructed from the building blocks of individual episodes.

What is memory?

Advertisements offering to improve your memory typically start by lowering your confidence in your ability to remember people's names and to reel off facts like the firm's sales figures. The assumption is that all this knowledge is stored away somewhere; the problem is how to activate it when required. In other words, passive knowledge has to be transformed into active memory. During most of the educational period of life there is a premium on remembering facts for tests and exams. But apart from actors and actresses who have to learn parts, and subjects in psychology memory experiments, there is not much call for precise verbal recall. There are useful mnemonics for remembering lists of unrelated facts; a famous one is *Richard of York Gave Battle in Vain* to remember the colours of the spectrum. One problem I have always found is how to remember the mnemonic in the first place. Some people find it easier to use their knowledge of the spectrum to generate the mnemonic, a case when the to-be-remembered fact itself becomes a mnemonic to aid memory for the Richard of York mnemonic! Memory improvement courses often suggest using similar mnemonic cues for remembering names and faces by forming a bizarre association between a name and a person's appearance. The fact that some people remember more autobiographical events than others, or are better at answering quiz questions, depends on relevant information being quickly retrieved. Certainly there is a premium on remembering useful information rather than simply regurgitating facts.

What it really comes down to is that in cognitive psychology the term memory is used in two rather different ways. The first refers to a passive memory store. All the information we have ever acquired, general knowledge of objects and categories and a permanent record of our personal experiences, are stored in long-term memory somewhere inside our heads. This definition of memory as a store underpins psychological models of long-term memory, semantic memory, autobiographical memory, episodic memory, short-term memory, each implying that different kinds of knowledge are parcelled out between various memory stores. In psychology experiments subjects can be presented with lists of words or pictures and asked to recall them after a few seconds (short-term memory) or after half an hour (long-term memory). In such experiments subjects know exactly what material needs to be recalled. Yet in daily life it is often difficult to decide which memories will be most useful in the current situation. It is not very helpful to recall that 'sharks are not birds' when you see a shark swimming towards you! In general there is all too wide a chasm between everything stored in passive memory and what we can actually remember at any one time. The common-sense definition of memory refers to our ability to recall facts when we need them. In other words, it refers to active memory in the sense of the memories which are currently available to us.

The shift towards a more active definition of memory in daily use was reflected in a parallel shift from short-term memory considered as a short-term store to the concept of working memory (Baddeley, 1986). Working memory is thought of as being a working space in which new inputs can be received and information from long-term memory can be retrieved. Working memory is necessary for cognitive functions which depend on an interaction between new and old information. Baddeley and his colleagues (reported in Baddeley, 1986; Hitch, 1978) carried out many experiments to demonstrate the role of working memory in reasoning, solving problems, mental arithmetic and reading. All these tasks, and most other cognitive activities, could not be performed at all if relevant information could not be held for a short period while it is being worked on. The emphasis of working memory research on active processing replaced the traditional concept of short-term memory as a passive store of to-be-remembered items, which had to be continually rehearsed if they were not to be forgotten.

Human working memory is limited in capacity but this is due, less to the length of time items are stored, than to a limitation on the number of things humans are able to consider simultaneously. It is for this reason that working memory has sometimes been equated with consciousness because we seem to be aware of problems we are working on, although often we cannot explain how we arrive at a solution. It is obvious that the contents of active working memory contain only a tiny subset of all the vast amount of passive knowledge available to us. Walking and talking, driving a car, carrying on polite conversations, all depend on prior experiences. Yet it would be odd to say that active working memory normally includes these automatic actions. However, the contents of active memory are constantly changing as we shift attention to the changing requirements of a situation. If I fall down in the street, I may have to call to mind the movements required to get up and walk.

One big question for cognitive psychology is to explain how we shift information between passive and active memory. How do we retrieve information into working memory just when we need it? I may not have thought about what to do if a fire bell rings for many years, yet out pops the relevant fire drill I learnt long ago. Schank (1982) discusses active memory in terms of being reminded of past events. He points out that people are constantly being reminded of earlier events and it is these that determine reactions to new events. If someone goes into a fast food restaurant, they may be reminded of a previous visit or of general expectations about the conventions for ordering and paying in such establishments. Being reminded in this way seems to proceed automatically (Mandler, 1985). We simply find that one experience leads us to think of something else and this activation of memory about a similar experience helps us to decide on an appropriate action.

In contrast to automatic reminding, Mandler describes the very different 'feel' when memories have to be retrieved by a conscious memory search, which is what most people mean by having a good or bad memory. When people are asked to rate their own memories, they usually refer to things like failing to remember people's names, forgetting where they read something, leaving a shopping list behind, failing to keep an appointment, finding you have walked home without posting a letter. Reason (1979) asked volunteers to keep a diary noting slips of action, the most common of which were repeating an action, like getting another clean cup out of the cupboard, or forgetting what one meant to do, like coming downstairs without bringing down a dirty cup. One thing you may have noticed about people's ratings of their own memories is that much of what people think of as memory is concerned with the future rather than the past. Memory for future intentions is termed *prospective* memory to differentiate it from *retrospective* memory for past events. (It is retrospective memory, of course, which has been investigated in the vast majority of psychological memory experiments.)

Harris (1984) reviewed some interesting experiments on prospective memory in which people had to remember to send postcards on certain days, or housewives had to remember to press a button – equivalent to taking a pill – at exact times during the day. Harris noted that people frequently use memory aids such as notes, shopping lists, tying knots in handkerchiefs. It is interesting, too, that the word 'remind' can be used to refer both to past events and to the future, as in 'remind me to ring my mother'. Memories in everyday life are a mixture of being automatically reminded of past events, conscious recall of the past – jokes, faces, names, childhood events – and memory for future plans. Memory is rarely a passive recall of events. Active memory is all to do with reminding, both of past and future events. The crucial issue is to explain why particular memories are activated in order to make sense of current experiences. Elaborate knowledge structures of categories and concepts are useless if relevant knowledge cannot be retrieved and used? If I see a dog in a restaurant, I might start wondering if dogs are usually allowed in, or perhaps be reminded that exceptions are made for a guide dog for a blind person. Knowledge that a dog is an animal and can breathe is unlikely to spring to my mind; the connection between dogs and fleas might!

Schema and frame representations

One general theory which has had a great deal of influence on models of how knowledge is used to guide interpretations of objects and events is schema theory. The basic idea, originally suggested by Bartlett (1932), is that human memory consists of high-level mental representations known as schemas, each of which encapsulates knowledge about everything connected with a class of objects or events. This notion has been taken up and expanded to cover many different situations. Examples are schemas for actions, like riding a bicycle, schemas for events, like going to a restaurant, schemas for situations, like working in an office, schemas for categories, like birds or mammals. In his 1932 book *Remembering* Bartlett was concerned with the role of schemas in influencing interpretations which are later recorded in memory. Discussing people's repeated memories of his famous 'War of the Ghosts' story, Bartlett made the point that, not only did they originally construe this rather bizarre Red Indian story to fit in with their own ideas of human relationships, but that this process continued to affect their later memories. Certainly many years after I first read the 'War of the Ghosts' as an undergraduate, my truncated memory of it included many of the points quoted by Bartlett.

Bartlett's explanation was that new inputs like the 'War of the Ghosts' story are incorporated into old schemas representing knowledge about the kinds of things that are likely to happen in folk tales. Schemas thus play a dual role: they represent general knowledge of objects and events and at the same time they guide the interpretation of newly occurring experiences which are eventually absorbed into general knowledge schemas. Bartlett gave an example of playing tennis. Knowledge of the rules of the game and a repertoire of strokes like backhands and volleys pre-exist as learned schemas. These schemas have a strong influence on reactions to a ball coming over the net but it would be a very poor tennis player who waved his racket in a previously determined direction regardless of where the ball bounces. Bartlett's view of the interaction between prior knowledge and incoming information from the environment is summarized in his statement that no action is completely new, nor is it completely old, but a mixture of the two. As a consequence of this interaction, any especially effective new strokes would become part of Bartlett's schema of actions, resulting in a gradual improvement of his tennis game. The importance of Bartlett's approach was that it emphasized the role of memory in building up a repository of experiences.

The main reason why Bartlett's schema theory was neglected for over forty years was that his description of schemas as knowledge representations suffered from a certain vagueness. How is the knowledge underlying the interpretation of a story, or the ability to play a backhand stroke in tennis, actually represented in memory? What mechanisms are responsible for applying knowledge schemas to new events and adapting them if necessary to circumstances? Minsky (1975) wrote a very influential article proposing a notation for representing schemas. Minsky called these knowledge representations 'frames' because he thought of them as frameworks for representing categories of objects and events. Frames consist of slots which can be filled in with appropriate values to represent situations. Figure 7 shows a frame to represent a simple schema representing knowledge of the concept 'dog'. The slots (shown as boxes in Figure 7) cover a wide range of information. For instance dogs are animals and usually have four legs, so these slots are filled in with specific values. So far this is very like any other semantic representation. In Collins and Quillian's network the concept 'dog' would be linked to the category 'animal' and have defining features like 'has four legs' and 'barks'.

Where frame representations differ crucially from semantic hierarchies and feature lists is that, instead of the features for each object being predefined, most of the slots in a frame are left empty. These are known as variables for the obvious reason that their contents are variable, although there is a range of possible optional values. A schema concept can be thought of being defined by fixed values, which are similar to the defining features which are supposed to be true of all dogs. In addition, there is a range of optional values which dogs may or may not have. Rather than having to indicate a fixed value for the size or colour of dogs, these features can be left vague until they are needed to describe a particular dog. The flexibility of frames makes them particularly suitable for dealing with the many different examples of a concept one is likely to encounter.

A frame guides the interpretation of an event by providing the types of slots relevant to dogs and the range of optional values which are appropriate. For example if you encounter a brown collie in a park, you can fill in the appropriate 'colour', 'type of dog' and 'location' slots to interpret that particular situation. This filled-in frame itself becomes the mental representation of that particular episode. At the same time, other slots in the frame for the 'dog' schema will stimulate inferences about the situation, for example is there an owner walking the dog? This may lead to the observation that it was my friend Bill who was walking the collie for its rich owner. Many of the slots in a frame

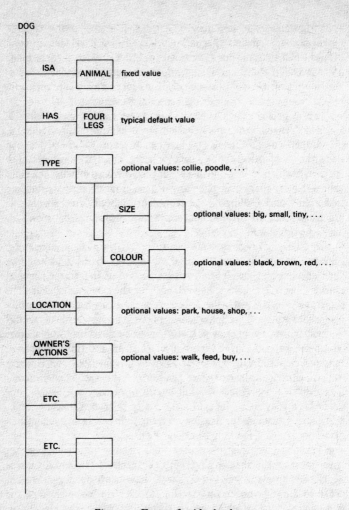

Figure 7 Frame for 'dog' schema.

invoke other schemas with frames of their own, such as events which are likely to occur in parks, or in shops, for example money changes hands. All this helps to make sense of situations in terms of inferences based on probable events.

A particularly useful aspect of frames is that, when specific information is lacking about slots, they can be filled in with what Minsky called default values. If no special feature is indicated, by default we select the most commonly expected value for a slot. If I say I am thinking of buying a dog, you would probably make the inference that I have in mind a medium-sized, non-dangerous, four-legged animal. Default values achieve the same kind of cognitive economy as inheritance does in hierarchical models, which allow you to assume that a dog can breathe because it is an animal. The *'isa* animal' slot in the dog frame means that all the default values for 'animnal' can be evoked to understand references to dogs breathing or drinking. For instance the sentence *My dog drinks a lot* would probably be interpreted as meaning that the dog drinks a lot of water. Default values represent typical features but they can be overriden by specific information. Thus the more specific information that my dog Fido drinks beer would be represented by inserting a specific value in the 'drinking' slot rather than the default value that animals usually drink water or milk. A frame which is filled in with nothing but default values can be thought of as a prototype representation (Johnson-Laird and Wason, 1977) since it will include all the typical features of a category. The default values for a typical bird will be characterized as having feathers, flying, being reasonably small, and so on. But if the frame is being used to describe an ostrich, then the 'activity' slot would need to be filled in with a specific value 'can't fly' which overrides the ordinary 'flying' default value for the bird frame.

Evaluation of frames for representing schemas

You may have been wondering what, if any, is the difference between a frame representation for a 'dog' schema as opposed to the other mental representations of concepts discussed in Chapter 3: 'dog' as a category in a semantic hierarchy, 'dog' as a set of defining features or 'dog' as a prototype defined by typical features. This is a difficult question to answer since, in principle, the same information can be included in all the representations to indicate semantic relations between concepts and features. 'Being walked in parks' could be a typical if not a defining feature of dogs.

Perhaps the most striking characteristic of a frame representation is the framework of slots waiting to be filled in with values relevant to the current situation. Since the frame itself supplies the representation of each particular situation, frames bridge the gap between semantic knowledge, as represented by the general frame for dogs, and representations of individual episodes involving dogs. Semantic knowledge, incorporated in the fixed values, default values and optional values for slots, determines representations of new episodes. But these new representations can also affect semantic memory by altering frames, for instance by acknowledging the possibility of three-legged dogs. Frames favour the inclusion of all sorts of information, for example events which occur when selling and buying dogs, as well as more conventional features like legs and tails. But the real beauty of frames is that default values are waiting in the wings ready to be called in only when required. Neither default values nor optional values have to be filled in if they are not relevant. If the topic of interest is the size of different breeds of dogs the 'location' slot may be ignored completely. This avoids the necessity to list all the features of a concept everytime it is recognized or mentioned.

Another general advantage of schemas is that they group objects together in ways that reflect natural real life experiences rather than simply listing features of objects like 'isa animal', 'has four legs', and 'barks'. Chairs and tables and food go naturally together in a restaurant frame. Chairs and tables and standard lamps go naturally together in a furniture shop. Chairs and tables and dogs may be a natural grouping in your sitting-room frame. It is easier, too, to visualize changing a slot as a result of learning from experiences, rather than having to reorganize an entire hierarchy of categories. It is simpler to erase dogs from my personal house frame than to alter their existence as canines in a semantic hierarchy. From all these points of view, frame representations for schemas are more flexible than predefined hierarchies of concepts and features. The information in frames is more geared towards the kinds of actions which would be appropriate in different situations.

However, before getting too carried away by the advantages of frames and schemas, I have to point out that the allocation of values to slots is really no more than an article of faith. It may seem easy enough to attribute a 'walking in a park' activity in a 'dog' frame designed for that purpose. However, complications immediately set in once one starts to take representations seriously. Unfortunately frame representations come up against many of the same problems as other semantic representations. Take the awkward ostrich again as an example. One possibility is for canaries and ostriches to appear as possible optional values in the 'type' slot of the bird frame (like collies and poodles in the dog frame in Figure 7). This means that, if the ostrich value is selected, a special note has to be made to override the fixed 'can fly' value in the bird frame. Alternatively an ostrich could be allocated a frame representation of its own with an *isa* slot pointing to 'bird'. The inclusion of a 'can't fly' fixed value in the ostrich frame would block the application of the more general 'flying' default value in the bird frame. The disadvantage is that there would have to be a frame for each type of bird or dog, each with its own set of slots and values. This would suffer from the same lack of cognitive economy as models which include feature lists for each concept.

In addition to the many difficulties involved in selecting appropriate slots within a frame, there is also a lot left to the imagination about the processes for calling up one schema rather than another. The 'dog' frame as a whole would be included in the 'animal' frame and in many other frames, for instance for 'pets' and 'parks'. Default values can be inherited only if an event has been allocated to a particular frame. It is only because *isa* animal is mentioned in the dog frame that it can be inferred that dogs breathe. If we were confronted with a toy dog, other frames would need to be activated like 'toys'. In fact the most disconcerting characteristic of all schema theories is the proliferation of information which can be triggered even by a simple concept like 'dog'. In principle there seems to be no limit to the potentially relevant facts one might be reminded of about dogs depending on the situation.

To demonstrate the flexibility of people's interpretations, think of the inferences you might make to interpret the presence of a dog in an antique shop, in a dog home, in a field of sheep, with a bow on its head. Did you think of a plaster dog, a pathetic mongrel, a fierce wolf-like dog or a gentle sheep dog, a spoilt pekinese probably belonging to a foolish middle-aged woman? If you did, you were exploiting default features of dogs you may not even have thought about for a long time. Note, too, the force of Minsky's (1975) remark that commonly accepted stereotyped default values can be counter-productive, leading people to see only what they expect to see. The dog with a bow on its head might have been in a surrealist painting. No matter what I say about dogs, a listener will try to infer which of all the possible values in the dog frame I am referring to. This potential for generating inferences has been called the inferential explosion.

All this mental flexibility has to be paid for. In the Collins and Quillian semantic hierarchy shown in Figure 4, the semantic relations between concepts and features are precisely specified. With the potentiality of frames for representing all types of situations, the crucial problem is how to limit the selection of relevant inferences. Interpretations of 'dog' episodes can be matched against different frames in different contexts, for example whether a plaster dog and a table are seen in an antiques shop or whether a man and his dog are walking around in the great outdoors looking for something to use as a picnic table. Of course, antique shops and picnics are also represented as frames with their own expected values. But if our minds are stuffed with frames depicting dogs and tables, picnics and ostriches, cabbages and kings, how do we recognize which frames provide a relevant context for other frames? The whole process appears to float on quicksand. Every identification of an object depends on the prior recognition of other objects and events. At what point do the frames stored inside our minds come into contact with reality?

All attempts to model the processes required to match new events against old knowledge have run into difficulties. Psychologists stress the importance of context for invoking relevant schemas. But they tend to treat the context as a given, forgetting that the contextual situation has to be interpreted in the first place. The context of a toyshop or the countryside can be recognized only by invoking 'toyshop' and 'countryside' frames. The presence of windows and trees are also frame representations. It might happen, too, that it is the appearance and activities – or lack of activity – of the 'dog' which helps to identify the contextual situation as a park or antique shop in the first place. I well remember the shock I got when a large unmoving dog in a local antique shop suddenly shifted its position, thus upsetting my initial interpretation of a 'wooden' model of a dog. The crux of the matter is that interpretations of the environment are necessary to provide the context for invoking relevant schemas. Yet these contextual interpretations are themselves dependent on schema representations. Inputs have to be interpreted in order to see whether they fit possible values in frames but these interpretations are supposed to be impossible without the help of contextual knowledge represented by other frames. Here we have a classic chicken and egg situation. To break out of this circularity what is needed is some way of identifying the situational context in the first place.

Representations of scripts and goals

The message so far is that one way of cutting down the inferential explosion of possible inferences is to build in a device for recognizing contextual situations and specifying the likely events and objects to be found there. Once a park scene has been identified as the location, the possible activities of dogs and owners can be limited to a circumscribed range of park-like activities. Minsky used the special term scenario for frame representations which describe locations and situations. This idea was extended by Roger Schank and his colleagues (Schank and Abelson, 1977) in the form of scripts which describe the contexts for routine events. A simplified version of the well-known 'Restaurant' script is shown in Figure 8.

Perhaps the best way to think about scripts is that they are large-scale frames which list variable slots for scenes and actions, actors and objects which you would expect in a prototype restaurant. Actual events which occur on a visit to a particular restaurant can be represented by filling in the slots for 'roles', 'props' and 'actions'. The sentence *When John Brown went to McDonalds he recognized one of the waitresses* would be interpreted by allocating McDonalds to the restaurant name slot, John Brown to the customer role and a friend to the waitress role. In the absence of any other information, it would be inferred from default values that John read the menu, ordered food, paid the bill and ended up less hungry but poorer than when he entered the restaurant.

Name: Restaurant

Props: Tables   *Roles*: Customer
        Menu   Waiter/waitress
        Food   Cook
        Bill   Cashier
        Tip   Owner

Entry conditions: *Results*:
Customer is hungry   Customer has less money
Customer has money   Customer is not hungry

Scene 1: *Entering*
        Customer enters restaurant
        Customer looks for table
        Customer goes to table
        Customer sits down

Scene 2: *Ordering*
        Waitress brings menu
        Customer reads menu
        Customer orders food
        Waitress gives food order to cook
        Cook prepares food

Scene 3: *Eating*
        Cook gives food to waitress
        Waitress brings food to customer
        Customer eats food

Scene 4: *Paying*
        Customer asks for bill
        Waitress gives bill to customer
        Customer gives tip to waitress
        Customer goes to cashier
        Customer gives money to cashier
        Customer leaves restaurant

Figure 8   Restaurant script.
Source: adapted from Bower, Black and Turner (1979).

Schank's theory was formalized as a knowledge-based computer program designed, like Quillian's theory, to comprehend language inputs. Whereas Quillian's knowledge base dealt with statements about categories and their properties (*A canary is a fish, An animal can breathe*), Schank's aim was to represent knowledge of situations so that his program could respond to a wide range of stories about natural events. The linguistic features of Schank's model will be discussed in Chapter 5. The issue of interest here is that, once a restaurant script has been identified as being relevant to an event, it constrains the interpretation of that event. A reference to a 'tip' will be understood as a financial reward in the paying scene of the restaurant script, rather than advice about bets on horse races, or a place for dumping rubbish. Scripts, then, fulfil the requirement of supplying a contextual framework in which some inferences and interpretations are appropriate and others are ruled out. Once John enters a restaurant, he doesn't even give a thought to the other possible meanings of 'tip'. If he sees a dog in a restaurant, his only consideration is about the health implications of the feature 'dogs have fleas', ignoring all other potential inferences about dogs. Frame representations at the script level provide the guidance necessary for matching slots for lower-level frames such as dogs and tables. As long as a script has been assigned, everything else falls into place. In this way the problem of prior recognition of a concept is bypassed by script assignment and the inferential explosion is curbed.

Of course, it is not always easy to identify the correct script context in the first place. In the absence of convenient statements like *John went to a restaurant*, each sequence of events has to be matched against possible scripts. In computer implementations of Schank's theory, the number of possible scripts has had to be restricted so as to aid script recognition. Otherwise, it may prove too difficult to decide whether a particular sequence of eating events fits a restaurant script or a picnic script. The problem is intensified when situations involve more than one script. For example different script representations would have to be activated to understand a situation in which a train journey script is suddenly broken into by a meal in a restaurant car script and later by an accident script. Schank and Abelson (1977) suggested that, after hearing a story in which several scripts are referred to, people will forget routine script events, unless they are especially relevant to the characters' goals, but unexpected happenings will be noted on a 'weird' list because they are likely to need further explanation.

It is interesting that script representations, which were motivated by the need for a contextual framework for interpreting individual frames, themselves turn out to require even larger-scale mental representations. Faced with a proliferation of possible interlocking scripts for representing a situation, Schank and others have argued that the only way to make sense of events is in terms of people's goals and intentions. Schank (1982) quotes a little story *John wanted to become king. He went to get some arsenic.* One thing that is virtually certain is that we do not have a 'killing kings' script. The situation can be comprehended only if we understand John's goal and make inferences based on likely actions he would be likely to contemplate in order to achieve his goal.

Further evidence for this level of analysis comes from 'remindings' which cut across script situations. Schank gives some amusing examples of real life reminding episodes which he collected from his colleagues. In one typical exchange between two Americans, one of them mentioned that his wife never cooked his steak as rare as he requested, which reminded the other American of how an English barber ignored his requests to cut his hair short enough. Cooking and hair-cutting scripts represent completely different sequences of actions and refer to contexts which would normally be kept quite separate. It was the similarity in specifying a goal (rare steak or short hair) each of which was frustrated by the failure of another person to respond which prompted the retrieval of the hair-cutting memory as being relevant to the telling of the steak story. Another example is the way the musical *West Side Story* 'reminds' people of *Romeo and Juliet* because of the similar goals and plans of the characters.

In later versions of his theory Schank (1982) took the line that people are unlikely to have their heads full of thousands of precompiled script routines for every possible event: dressing in the morning, catching a bus, travelling on a train, or aeroplane, going to the hairdresser, to the doctor, to the dentist, and so on.

This was confirmed by an experiment by Bower, Black and Turner (1979) in which subjects tended to muddle up events from similar script-based stories. An example is not being sure whether a description had been about the waiting-room in a 'dentist' or 'doctor' story. It was on the basis of such evidence that Schank suggested that knowledge is not stored in the form of set sequences of script actions for each individual event. Rather than information about waiting-rooms and paying bills being included in many different scripts, cognitive economy would be achieved by storing these as separate knowledge representations. Schank called these knowledge representations Memory Organization Packets (MOPs), defining them as 'packets' of information about objects and situations. People would then be able to draw on these representations of knowledge in order to understand situations. Instead of being prestored as individual scripts, knowledge of likely events, goals and plans would be brought together to create a script-like representation whenever this is required. In order to interpret a particular visit to a restaurant or a doctor, general MOPs about paying bills as well as MOPs specific to restaurants and doctors would be retrieved in order to construct a superscript for that particular occasion. As you may have realized, Memory Organization Packets are just a new name for schemas, which were defined as representing knowledge about classes of objects and events.

Schank developed this notion of creating scripts on demand as part of a theory of dynamic memory. Instead of a rigid distinction between semantic memory, incorporating general knowledge, and episodic memory for personal experiences, Schank suggests that memories are stored at many levels ranging from the most specific to the most general. Each time I visit a doctor I record the particular events of that episode in 'event memory' – equivalent to episodic memory. Soon the particular details of that visit will be forgotten and merged into a memory for a generalized event like 'visiting health professionals'. In fact I am unlikely to notice a lot about events in waiting-rooms on future visits, assuming that they carry on predictably as before. Eventually knowledge about situations becomes even more general and can be subsumed under a person's overall intentions and goals. For instance, an 'eating' goal may be served by visiting a favourite restaurant or by buying some food in a shop or by looking up the *Good Food Guide*.

In his theory of memory Schank took seriously the gradual transformation of episodes into general schemas and the role of generalized knowledge in interpreting new events. But it is easier to state the problem than to work out a precise notation for representing the mechanisms responsible for being reminded of relevant knowledge representations. As with all frame-like representations, the major problem in analysing an event or story is to decide which of all the many possible mental representations are relevant to its interpretation. The whole reminding process requires the ability to switch from one schema representation to another, to appreciate that some earlier experience of an encounter with a fierce dog may be relevant to dealing with an angry customer in a restaurant. What is needed is a system which allows for different schemas to be accessed in response to new inputs from the environment.

Recognizing new inputs

Although every cognitive psychologist pays lip service to the interaction between top-down processing, based on prior knowledge, and bottom-up processing, based on new inputs from the environment, the enterprise of modelling the interactions is extremely difficult. It is not easy to allow for apparently limitless flexibility in the exploitation of memories for past experiences and, at the same time, to provide an account of the precise mechanisms involved. For one thing there is the danger that too much reliance on knowledge representations and expectations about probable events may lead to seeing only what we expect to see, what Minsky (1975) referred to as over-reliance on default value prototypes. If I expect to see the furniture which is normally in my 'sitting-room' frame, I may simply not be able to make the inferences necessary to recognize the panther which has climbed in through my window. There is nothing in the 'house' frame which is likely to remind me of zoo animals. In fact since 'pets' may form part of a 'house' frame, I might be misguided enough to categorize the ferocious panther as a potential pet.

If you think about it carefully, the whole reminding process relies on recognizing objects and events in the first place. Sighting the panther ought to have reminded me of stories about wild animals escaping from zoos, but this depends on the ability to identify the unexpected object in the first place. It seems, then, that some kind of preliminary input representation is necessary which can be compared with expectations arising from knowledge representations. It is not within the scope of this book to describe the perceptual processes involved in 'seeing' and 'hearing' visual and acoustic signals from the environment (see Sanford, 1985, Barber, 1987). Here it is necessary to note only that the product of the visual system must be in a form which can be matched against knowledge representations already stored in the mind.

Let us flesh this point out with some examples. In order to respond to dogs as pets and panthers as wild animals, perceptual representations of these objects need to be mapped on to knowledge representations in memory like *A dog is a pet animal* and *A panther is a dangerous wild animal*. Recognition of objects will depend on identifying features in the environment which can be categorized as typical of dogs or panthers. Frame-type representations are particularly designed for matching events against expected situations. If a brown collie in a park matches the optional slots in a 'dog' frame, it will be recognized as a typical 'doggy' episode. If a person enters a building, sits down and orders food from a piece of paper, this matches the entering and ordering slots of the restaurant script shown in Figure 8. If I see an object in a restaurant with panther-like features, this may remind me of some quite unusual frames, with slots for escapes from zoos, or painted decorations. The point is that I have to recognize the panther-like features *before* I can get started on selecting an appropriate frame. For pattern matching to occur, there must be two representations to match, one representation of inputs from the actual environment and the other a mental representation of a concept or schema.

I do not mean to imply that it is necessary to have a fully fledged image of a dog or a panther before knowledge-based expectations come into play. As Neisser (1976) was one of the first to emphasize, recognition of objects depends on what he called a 'perceptual cycle' (see Figure 9). This cycle allows for

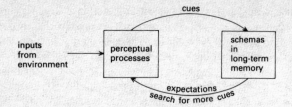

Figure 9 The perceptual cycle.
Source: adapted from Neisser (1976).

continual interaction between analysis of perceptual features and retrieval of knowledge schemas. Neisser's suggestion was that fast perceptual processes produce a preliminary and temporary representation of input features which act as cues to activate knowledge schema representations, which in turn can direct attention to a more detailed analysis of cue features. Neisser termed his model analysis-by-synthesis to reflect the interplay between analysis of cue features and synthesis of interpretations based on knowledge. The circularity of the process ensures that perceptions are accurate, as a result of checking perceptual cues and being guided by expectations. This is in contrast to the linear transfer of information from one box to another in Figure 1 in Chapter 1.

Neisser's ideas have proved influential as a way of posing the interaction between bottom-up analysis of inputs and top-down guidance from knowledge schemas. But it has not proved easy to specify the nature of the temporary representations of inputs which can be interpreted in the light of prior knowledge. The problem is that processing at this level appears to be automatic and outside conscious awareness. What do 'panther' features look like just *before* an object is recognized as a panther? What exact features in the environment trigger the activation of the 'walking a brown collie in the park' slots of a dog frame or a 'Waiter, there's a fly in my soup' episode in a restaurant script?

Conclusions

I started by emphasizing that representations of knowledge are useful only to the extent that they are actively available for interpreting events and planning actions, and in turn are amenable to change in the light of environmental feedback from the consequences of actions. The tenor of the discussion has led to the notion that this depends on automatic activation of similar past experiences, in other words, being actively reminded of relevant knowledge. However, because the content of each person's knowledge is idiosyncratic depending on the exact pattern of their past experiences, psychological theories have tended to concentrate on the structure of how general knowledge is organized, whether as semantic hierarchies, feature lists, prototypes or frame representations for schemas and scripts. One problem is that humans are so adaptable that they can utilize knowledge of all the types suggested. If asked whether canaries can breathe, they refer to the default values for animals. If asked to produce lists of typical features for tables and furniture, they respond as expected. So experimental investigations tend either to oversimplify behaviour or to be overwhelmed by the wealth of human knowledge.

Human beings find it relatively easy to access relevant information to understand what is going on around them. They are unlikely to confuse real dogs and toy dogs. They know whether they are watching a soap opera or an everyday scene. They appreciate the different contexts which would affect the interpretation of *What a tip!* In general, perceptions are both accurate and relevant. It is only under extremely adverse conditions, physical or mental, that people totally misperceive objects in the environment. When people do misinterpret events, it is usually in the sense of misunderstanding other people's motives, or relying too much on social expectations based on strongly held beliefs.

All these issues really boil down to the intractable problem of specifying links between general semantic knowledge and individual experiences. It seems reasonable enough that people should recognize a three-legged dog by analogy with the known features of the dog schema. But this is a case where it would *not* be sensible to alter the value of the 'four legs' slot in a permanent frame representation for dogs. On the other hand, being told about a hitherto unknown breed of dog would be a useful bit of new information to store in memory. Equally I might stick with the typical script of restaurant events even if my most recent experiences were of the fly in my soup variety. Somehow personal experiences of idiosyncratic objects and events are able to coexist with commonly accepted general knowledge. Since general knowledge is obviously built up from many individual past experiences, the resulting mix is not easy to explain.

The above discussion does not mean that nothing has been learned about active memory. In fact it might reasonably be claimed that it is only now that the right questions are being asked about the two-way interactions between knowledge representations and the way the environment is experienced and acted upon. Some of these are summarized below.

1 What factors affect the retrieval of passive knowledge into active memory?
2 What accounts for the automatic reminding process by which past experiences are seen to be relevant to current events?
3 On what basis are frame representations of schemas adapted to interpret individual, possibly idiosyncratic, episodes?
4 How are contextual situations recognized and what effect does this have on the interpretation of actions and events?
5 What principles govern the interaction between the analysis of features necessary for accurate perception and the activation of knowledge representations necessary for recognition of objects and events?

5

Language and knowledge

In previous chapters interpretations of the environment have been shown to be dependent on cognitive representations of the world, whether these are formulated as semantic networks, feature lists, schemas or scripts. But what is the role in all this of language? One of the most common actions of human beings is to talk. We also understand other people's communications, and can perceive and interpret sounds and written letters. A natural question for a cognitive psychologist concerns the knowledge representations necessary to use and understand language. In this chapter I shall be considering the knowledge that underlies our ability to use and understand language.

What is language?

Language is as hard as thinking or memory to pin down. It is pervasive in human knowledge and action at all levels. In the first place, language influences the way people interpret the environment. Without going into the details of the Sapir-Whorf linguistic relativity hypothesis (which states that people's actual perceptions of the world are determined by the language they speak), it is indisputable that interpretations of experiences are influenced by the way they are described. If I am told that a table is a genuine antique, or that it is a fake, my behaviour towards it may be very different. Reading a list of instructions or perusing a travel brochure will affect future plans; the way a lecturer puts over a topic may determine how much a student later recalls of the subject matter. A great deal of knowledge is initially presented verbally, particularly knowledge which is learnt from teachers and books. In addition to learning from other people's speech and writing, thinking often takes the form of a kind of internal conversation with ourselves. Psychologists acknowledge the importance of this internal mediating role of language, particularly in explaining the development of thought in children (e.g. Vygotsky, 1962).

Language is the basis for communicating information, both in immediate face-to-face conversations and in the longer-lasting form of written records. It is virtually impossible to imagine what modern life would be like if we were suddenly cut off from all verbal knowledge. Instead of being told what things are and reading about past discoveries, each generation would have to learn everything from scratch. In order to pass information from one generation to the next, non-literate societies develop oral traditions of story-telling. Individuals learn by heart sagas and lists of customs and laws which they can recite to succeeding generations. Yet despite this universal drive for communication, there is the paradoxical fact that there are many thousands of different human languages, each of which is an impenetrable barrier to free communication. Groups of native speakers are locked within the confines of their own language. Except for true bilinguals, most of us are all too aware of the difficulties of learning a new language.

One big difference between languages you know and languages you don't know is that it is not at all easy to 'hear' your native language in the same way that you hear other languages. With languages you don't know you can, for instance, describe what Turkish or Russian 'sounds' like, soft and sibilant or harsh and angular. You have only to listen to speakers of a language you are not familiar with to realize the difficulty of picking out from the stream of sounds where one word begins and another ends. But it is virtually impossible to stand back and consider what English sounds like (Fodor, 1983). The sounds and letters of your own language are transparent; the meaning leaps out directly from the printed marks on a page. And yet the relation between sounds and meanings is arbitrary in all languages, including English. There is no reason why the sound *basket* should mean a receptacle made of cane, rather than the sound *panier* in French, or *sepet* in Turkish. Yet to English speakers *basket* has an obvious meaning rather than being a combination of random sounds. So the first issue for any theory of language to explain is why the connections between arbitrary sounds and meanings seem so obvious in languages we know but are so conspicuously absent in languages we don't know.

The knowledge of language speakers needs to encompass a wide range of skills. They have to be able to use the correct vocabulary, recognize words, speak grammatically and idiomatically, understand other speakers and read written texts. The emphasis of most psychological theories has been on the comprehension of linguistic inputs, rather than on the production of utterances and the writing of texts. The reason is simple. It is relatively easy to present to a person – or to a computer – spoken utterances and typewritten inputs and then to test whether these have been correctly understood. It is more problematic to infer what might be going on inside someone's head just before they decide to say or write something. Furthermore, researchers into language fall into two camps, those who concentrate on the linguistic knowledge which characterizes language users, and those who emphasize the use of language for communication. In this chapter I shall be concentrating on theories about the linguistic knowledge and processes necessary for using language at all; in the next chapter on the use of language for its primary purpose of communication.

Language as verbal responses

Given the concentration of the behaviourists on animal behaviour, it is perhaps somewhat ironic that one of the earliest proponents of speech as active responses was the well-known behaviourist

B. F. Skinner. Skinner's book *Verbal Behaviour* (1957) was a virtuoso attempt to explain language without taking into account any 'mentalistic' events such as ideas, meanings, grammatical rules, or even anything corresponding to the statement that someone can speak English. From Skinner's point of view, verbal utterances consist of individual combinations of random sounds. The idea is that the first sounds a child happens to emit can be shaped up by reinforcement to blossom into the full range of utterances exhibited by an adult. Skinner gives a few examples of how verbal responses might come to be conditioned, responses which he claims to classify, not because of what they mean, but solely as a function of the stimulus–response contingencies in which they happened to occur. What he calls a 'mand' is the result of a need stimulus (for example a need for salt) to which a response *Pass the salt* might happen to be emitted, followed by the reinforcement of being handed some salt. A 'tact' occurs when the stimulus input is an object like, say, an iceberg, to which the response *That's an iceberg* is followed by the reinforcement *That's right*. The motivation in this case, Skinner suggests, is the usefulness for parents of having 'tacting' children rushing around telling them what things are. Skinner goes on to apply this technique to a bewildering variety of linguistic behaviour, the flavour of which you can get only by reading *Verbal Behaviour*. Skinner's analysis carries you along in an outrageously plausible manner, stretching to such delightful flights of fancy as explaining Robert Browning's *Home Thoughts From Abroad*.

Oh, to be in England
Now that April's there

as a 'magical mand', presumably based on the success of *Oh, to be* statements in obtaining rewards in the past.

It is only when you stop to consider the theory that several points hit you. First, it is only for the very simplest cases that Skinner spells out precise stimulus–response–reinforcement contingencies. For the rest he relies on looking at utterances with the 'form most characteristic of mands' – a direct appeal to types of sentences which is just what he eschewed in the first place. Second, very little verbal behaviour takes the form of mands and tacts, or the other echoic and textual copying responses on which Skinner spends so much space. Most language verbalizations are examples of what Skinner calls 'intraverbal responses', as when you say something and I reply. Perhaps it is not surprising that Skinner skates rather quickly over this type of response since there are enormous difficulties in explaining all the thousands of verbal responses that can be made to verbal inputs. Apart from the fact that none of these is likely to occur regularly enough to get reinforced very often, it is an uphill task to explain people's utterances as if they were equivalent to a rat pressing a bar to obtain a food reward, ignoring totally the meanings of the sounds being uttered.

It is true that Skinner's theory of verbal behaviour has become a straw man which it is all too easy to attack. Moreover, the verbal learning experiments carried out in the 1950s and 1960s did not even address the question of natural language use. Consequently there was a fallow period for psychological studies of language until the impact of Noam Chomsky's theory of transformational grammar.

Language as linguistic rules

Noam Chomsky is a linguist whose writings first came to the attention of psychologists in the form of a vitriolic review (1959) of Skinner's *Verbal Behaviour*. The main burden of Chomsky's complaint was that speakers can understand and respond to an infinite number of sentences. Since, apart from a few ritualized greetings, the vast majority of word combinations are novel and have never been heard before, there is no way even in principle that they could have been emitted as past utterances and rewarded as claimed by Skinner. In addition, if utterances are subject to the rewards an individual happens to obtain, everybody's use of language will be slightly different depending on which combinations of sounds happened to be reinforced by other people. Instead Chomsky put forward the view that language consists of a set of rules which enable speakers to produce an infinite number of possible grammatical sentences. In other words, a language exists as a linguistic entity before a child starts to learn it. This is exactly the opposite of Skinner's belief that what we call language is the result of a succession of essentially arbitrary reinforcements of some utterances rather than others.

Chomsky's (1957) transformational grammar was formulated as a set of explicit syntactic rules for generating all the grammatical sentences in English but ruling out non-grammatical sequences of words. Some very simple rules are shown in Figure 10. These rules take the form of 'rewriting' or expanding linguistic symbols in such a way that they reveal the grammatical relationships between phrases and words in sentences. For instance the first rule states that a sentence includes a noun phrase (NP) and a verb phrase (VP). The next four rules state that a noun phrase (NP) can be rewritten as a noun (rule 2) or as an article and a noun (rule 3) or as an adjective and a noun (rule 4) or as a pronoun (rule 5). The rules at the end (rules 8 to 12) allow syntactic categories like noun (N), verb (V), adjective, article and pronoun to be rewritten as actual words. Examples of these rules would be that a noun phrase could take the form of *Jane* (rule 2), *the boy* (rule 3), *good apples* (rule 4) or *she* (rule 5).

These rules are called phrase structure rules because they generate syntactic phrase structure 'parsings' for sentences. For instance if rules 1, 2, 8, 6, 9, 3, 11 and 8 are applied in sequence, they generate the phrase structure for the sentence shown in the 'tree' diagram in Figure 11. You can work out for yourself, though, that these same simplified rules can be used to generate a phrase structure for the ungrammatical combination of words

1	S (sentence)	→ NP (noun phrase) + VP (verb phrase)
2	NP	→ N (noun)
3	NP	→ article + N
4	NP	→ adjective + N
5	NP	→ pronoun
6	VP	→ V (verb) + NP
7	VP	→ V + *adjective*
8	N	→ *Jane, boy, girl, apples*
9	V	→ *likes, hit, was hit, was, are cooking, are*
10	adjective	→ *good, unfortunate*
11	article	→ *a, the*
12	pronoun	→ *he, she, they*

Figure 10 Simplified version of Chomsky's (1957) phrase structure rules.

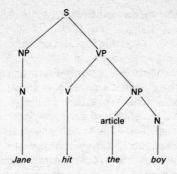

Figure 11 Syntactic tree structure for a grammatical sentence.

shown in the syntactic tree structure in Figure 12. To block this, it would be necessary to add all sorts of extra rules stating that compatible subjects and verbs have to be selected. These would include syntactic rules that *Jane* should not be followed by a plural verb and semantic rules to indicate the improbability of the fact that Jane would be cooking the boy – unless she was a cannibal. Chomsky's later writings were much taken up with tricky questions of how to rule out syntactically and semantically anomalous sentences.

In the late 1950s the psychological influence of Chomsky's theory was enormous. His claim that it is linguistic knowledge

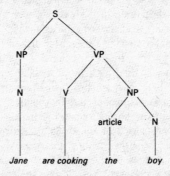

Figure 12 Syntactic tree structure for an ungrammatical sentence.

which accounts for a native speaker's ability to produce and understand language was one of the main spurs to the development of psychologists' concern with knowledge representations. In the case of language, Chomsky's rules supplied psychologists with a ready-made set of representations for linguistic knowledge. Particularly influential was the notion that understanding language entails mapping the surface order of the words in a sentence into some 'deeper' representation. To see why this is so, I will quote one or two of Chomsky's own examples. The sentence *Visiting aunts can be a nuisance* has just the one 'surface structure' order of words. But this sentence has two possible meanings: 'To visit aunts is a nuisance' or 'Aunts who visit are a nuisance'. These can be represented as two different grammatical 'deep structures': the first indicating that *aunts* is the object of the verb *visit*, the second that *aunts* is the subject of the verb *visit*. In contrast, consider two sentences which have quite different surface structures: *John kicked the cat* and *The cat was kicked by John*. Despite the different surface order of words, both these sentences map on to a virtually identical deep structure, which represents the fact that it is *John* who is the subject of the verb *kicked*.

It was in order to represent these aspects of language that Chomsky introduced transformational rules to convert 'deep structures' into 'surface structures' and vice versa. One example is a passive transformation which would re-order words so as to 'transform' the deep structure underlying *John kicked the cat* into the passive surface word order *The cat was kicked by John*. The basic idea was that deep structures are available for semantic interpretation while surface structures provide the information needed to turn the surface order of words into actual sounds. Chomsky (1965) was interested in the relationship between sounds at one end of the linguistic process and the interpretation of meanings at the other, as shown in Figure 13.

Deep structures are generated in the first place by 'phrase structure' rules of the kind given in Figure 10. It is the subject/verb/object relationships in the deep structure *Jane hit the boy* from which the meaning can be interpreted by the semantic interpretation rules in the semantic component. The transformational rules convert these deep structures into surface structure word orders like *The boy was hit by Jane*. It is the surface

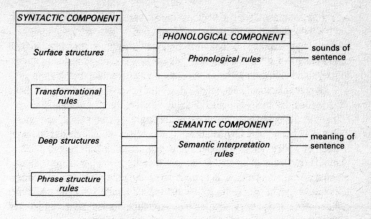

Figure 13 Chomsky's (1965) theory of language.

structure *The boy was hit by Jane* which can be input to phonological rules for producing the actual sounds of the sentence in the right order.

The crux of Chomsky's theory is that the syntactic component is central to the transformation of sounds into meanings. It is the transformational rules in the syntactic component which perform the important function of mapping the sounds of utterances on to their meanings. Chomsky's concern is with the grammar of a language, even though syntax is interpreted far more widely than traditional grammars learnt at school. A further assumption of his model is that the syntactic analysis of surface structures and deep structures must be completed before semantic interpretation can come into play. The separation of syntactic analysis and semantic analysis is an important postulate of Chomsky's theory.

Chomsky's theory seemed to offer psychologists a perfect model of the knowledge required to speak a language. As shown in Figure 13, Chomsky's theory proposed that the syntactic component 'transforms' deep structures into surface structures. Chomsky, being a linguist, conceived his theory as representing syntactic relationships which explain the linguistic competence of all language speakers. Psychologists, however, took his theory as implying that deep 'meaningful' structures are transformed into surface structure word orders as part of the performance of actually producing utterances. Conversely the surface order of words have to be 'detransformed' into deep structures in the process of understanding sentences. It is only after this syntactic analysis is complete that semantic interpretation can begin.

The revelation that language abilities might take the form of rules for generating and understanding sentences caused a flurry of psycholinguistic experiments throughout the 1960s and early 1970s. These experiments attempted to test the idea that people will take more time to understand sentences which require many transformations. For instance active sentences require few if any transformations to convert them from surface structures to deep structures. The deep structure and the surface structure of *John chased the girl* are very similar because the active sentence directly represents the deep structure syntactic relationships between *John* as subject and *the girl* as object. Taking their cue from the earlier version of Chomsky's theory (1957), psychologists like Miller and McKean (1964) proposed that, in order to generate more complex sentences like passives, negatives and passive negatives, active sentences had to undergo one or more passive and negative transformations. Similarly the surface structure of a passive sentence like *The girl was chased by John* would need to be 'detransformed' into its equivalent deep structure, *John chased the girl*.

The main experimental methodology was sentence verification, in which subjects had to respond 'true' or 'false' depending on whether a sentence correctly described a situation in a picture. An example would be the spoken sentence *The boy kicked the girl* followed by a picture of a girl kicking a boy (for some unexplained reason many of the sentences in the early experiments tended to depict rather violent situations). The prediction was that subjects would take longer to verify the truth or falsity of complex sentences like passives, negatives and passive negatives which require syntactic transformations, as compared with active 'kernel' sentences which were supposed to need only minimal transformations. The general, perhaps not too surprising, result was that complex sentences like *The boy was not chased by the dog* took longer to verify than simple active sentences like *The boy chased the dog*. However, what was surprising and unexpected was that this held true only when all other things were equal.

Unfortunately, among the other things which were *not* equal, were variations in the meanings of the sentences. In most of the experiments sentences were used which referred to situations in which both versions of a sentence are possible. For example *The cat is chasing the dog* is just as likely, well almost as likely, as *The dog is chasing the cat*. But in a classic experiment Slobin (1966) included some sentences which referred to an irreversible situation, for example *The flowers are being watered by the girl* where the reversed situation *The girl is being watered by the flowers* is nonsensical. Slobin found that with normal 'reversible' sentences, judgements about passives were, as expected, slower than actives. But with irreversible sentences, subjects took no longer to verify passive sentences than active sentences. Thus the passive sentence *The flowers are being watered by the girl* was just as easy to deal with as the active sentence *The girl is watering the flowers*. In fact responses to all the non-reversible sentences were considerably faster than those to reversible sentences, even for anomalous sentences like *The girl is being watered by the flowers*. This was presumably because subjects could easily judge the truth or falsity of a sentence on the basis that the only plausible situation was a picture of a girl watering flowers. Other experiments supported the finding that semantic plausibility influences judgements about sentences (Wason, 1965; Herriot, 1969; Greene, 1970).

The difficulty for Chomsky was that, according to the model shown in Figure 13, the syntactic component is supposed to be isolated from semantic interpretations of probable meanings. The semantic knowledge that flowers don't usually water girls should have no effect on the syntactic process of detransforming the surface word order of *The girl is being watered by the flowers* into its deep structure *The flowers are watering the girl*. It is only after the deep structure has been passed on to the semantic component that the semantic anomaly should be spotted. This muddying of the clear syntactic hypothesis was cited as evidence against Chomsky's theory that syntactic analysis has to be completed before semantic analysis of meanings can begin. The subjects in Slobin's experiment seemed to be using semantic information to aid the comprehension of syntactically complex sentences like *The flowers are not being watered by the girl*. It can be argued (Garnham, 1985) that the semantic effect might take place *after* a sentence has been syntactically analysed. The problem is how to disentangle syntactic analysis and semantic comprehension. In sentence verification experiments response times are recorded from the time when the sentence and picture are presented until the subject presses a 'true' or 'false' button. It is therefore impossible to separate out the time taken for pure syntactic analysis and the time taken for semantic decisions about whether the sentence matches the situation shown in the picture. Certainly as far as this line of psycholinguistic research was concerned, these results were interpreted as meaning that it was no longer possible to demonstrate an isolated stage of purely linguistic analysis, uncontaminated by consideration of probable meanings, as required by Chomsky's theory of linguistic competence.

Chomsky's response to these experimental results was to take the line that his theory of transformational grammar defines the linguistic competence of an 'idealized' native speaker. Performance, as displayed in psychological experiments and in natural slips and errors, cannot be used as evidence to contradict a coherent grammatical theory. Furthermore, in view of the proliferation of syntactic rules required to rule out ungrammatical sequences of words, a constant feature of Chomsky's writings (1965, 1981) has been the difficulty of explaining how children are able to learn an exceedingly complex set of linguistic rules before they can start talking grammatically. Chomsky's explanation is that there must be a small number of general principles common to all languages – linguistic universals – which limit the number of possible linguistic rules. If these general rules are innately wired-in to the genetic structure of all humans, this would reduce to manageable proportions the task for each child of learning the complexities of their own particular language. Chomsky has continued his work in linguistics by attempting to reduce the number of transformational rules to a few very general principles which constrain the structures of all languages. One consequence of the search for abstract universal principles is that linguistic research has tended to move further and further from the details of how humans extract meanings from utterances in a particular language. After reading the later versions of Chomsky's theory, one would be no nearer to knowing how to specify the actual rules for any particular language, even the English in which his books are written. This is the main reason why, after the honeymoon period of psycholinguistics in the 1960s and 1970s, psychologists and linguists have tended to go their own ways.

This dividing of the ways has led to a bewildering diversity of approaches to language use. Some psychologists have pursued the search for psychological mechanisms for transforming sentences into deep structures; others have concentrated on the semantic content of utterances; others on the role of general knowledge in interpretations; others take for granted speakers' linguistic knowledge and are more concerned with commitments to communication. An important point to note is that these are all legitimate areas of research which illuminate one or other aspect of the remarkable human ability to use and understand language.

Language as parsing strategies

During the 1970s several psychologists (Bever, 1970; Kimball, 1973) proposed sets of parsing strategies for exploiting cues in the surface order of words to extract deep syntactic relationships between the words and phrases in a sentence. These psychologists accepted Chomsky's aim of transforming surface word order into deep syntactic structures. But rather than sticking to purely linguistic rules, they were more interested in psychological strategies designed to explain why humans find some sentences more difficult to understand than other sentences.

Another characteristic of these theories was their attempt to model the analysis of utterances word by word. Theories of linguistic competence like Chomsky's operate on the overall structures of whole sentences. In Figure 11 the structure of the whole sentence is displayed before the individual words are inserted at the bottom of the phrase structure tree. From common observation it is pretty obvious that people do not wait to hear an entire sentence before they begin to wonder what it means. For this reason psychological models of human language concentrated on building up syntactic representations on the basis of the first one or two words in a sentence. In contrast to the full grammatical analysis possible in linguistic theories, psychological parsing strategies had to be formulated as hunches which might have to be altered as a sentence progressed. To give you the flavour of this approach, three typical parsing strategies were:

1 In any sentence the first clause with a Noun–Verb (Noun) sequence is the main clause, unless it is marked as a subordinate clause by a subordinating conjunction, for example *while, because, although*.
2 Any Noun–Verb–Noun sequence should be interpreted as Actor–Action–Object.
3 Whenever you find a word, like *on* or *for* or *to*, assume that the next phrase will be more than one word.

Given the sentence *John hit the girl although he knew he shouldn't* parsing strategy 1 would analyse the first four words as the main clause. But in a sentence like *Although John hit the girl he knew he shouldn't* the presence of the word *although* would trigger an alternative analysis that the first five words of the sentence should be parsed as a subordinate clause. Parsing strategy 2 is responsible for interpreting 'deep structure' meaning relationships. For instance the sequence *John* (Noun) *hit* (Verb) *the girl* (Noun) would be parsed as *John* (Actor), *hit* (Action) *the girl* (Object). Parsing strategy 3 lists a class of words, which typically introduce prepositional phrases like *on the waterfront, to the shop*.

Clark and Clark (1977) pointed out some of the difficulties in specifying such parsing strategies. For one thing, in English there are many words like *to* and *that* which can introduce several different types of clauses, for example *to London, to eat an egg, I know that she loves that man*. If surface word cues are ambiguous, parsing strategies will need to become increasingly complex to deal with all possible interpretations. Both the arch-rivals, Skinner and Chomsky, and anyone else who has attempted to list all the rules and exceptions of a natural language, have run into this complexity problem. For instance in English it is by no means an easy task to tell a foreigner when it is correct to use *a* or *the*, as in *A tiger is the most fearsome of beasts* versus *The tiger is a fearsome beast*. This is, after all, why it is so difficult to teach or learn a new language.

One way of dealing with ambiguous word-by-word parsing strategies is to postpone a decision about the correct syntactic structure until more words have been analysed. Thus if the word *to* is followed by a noun phrase, it is likely to be a preposition, as in *to London*, or *to the shop*; if it is followed by a verb, it is more likely to be part of a verb phrase, as in *to boil an egg* or *to go to London*. Sometimes, too, it may be necessary to pay attention to semantic plausibility. Consider for instance the three following sentences which demonstrate some of the strategic decisions that are likely to affect semantic interpretations.

1 John figured that Susan wanted to take the cat out.
2 John figured that Susan wanted to take the train to New York out.
3 John and Susan saw the Rocky Mountains flying to California.

In sentence 1 people assume that *take* and *out* go together rather than *figured* and *out* because the words *take* and *out* are closer together. Sentence 2 is hard to interpret because there is nothing else to go with *out* except *figured* and yet *figured* and *out* are so far apart. However, in sentence 3 no one assumes that *the Rocky Mountains* and *flying* go together for obvious semantic reasons although the words are so near to each other in the sentence. All these examples militate against a clean set of syntactic parsing strategies which can operate without taking into account the possible meanings of sentences. This is, of course, in direct opposition to Chomsky's 1965 theory in which syntactic analysis and semantic analysis are kept quite distinct (see Figure 13).

As I have already hinted, while psychological models of parsing may work for the simple sentences quoted by their authors, no one has worked out how they would apply to the whole range of English sentences, much less all the unfinished, not totally grammatical utterances we so often produce in speech. Humans are so good at understanding language that it is all too easy to appeal to linguistic intuitions in support of parsing strategies like those discussed above.

Language as computer programs

One community of researchers who have persevered with rule-based parsing models are 'artificial intelligence' researchers writing computer programs designed to understand human languages. From the first unsuccessful attempts at machine translation in the 1940s, language has seemed a natural for computer programs. If questions and statements are typed in and the computer responds with an answer or a summary, this is taken as showing that the program has understood the input. Since language is such a peculiarly human ability, the hope is that a program incorporating rules which mimic language understanding will inevitably throw light on the rules and operations humans use to extract meanings from language inputs. Several famous computer programs (for example Weizenbaum's ELIZA, 1966; Winograd's SHRDLU, 1972; Schank's SAM, 1975) are described in some detail in Greene (1986).

Basically natural language computer programs can be thought of as implementations of the psychological parsing strategies discussed above, with the crucial difference that computers are quite literally dumb. Unlike humans, computers have no built-in linguistic intuitions to tell them that *to* should be treated as a preposition in *I went to London* but as part of a verb in *I went to buy clothes*. As far as the computer is concerned, the letters *t* and *o* are meaningless symbols until the programmer inputs some instructions about how they should be combined and interpreted. Consequently all the rules necessary for language understanding have to be explicitly articulated by the researcher so that they can be formulated as program instructions for constructing an interpretation of a sentence as the words are input one by one.

Interestingly the computer syntactic parsing programs soon ran into the same problems as their psychological counterparts. Because of the inherent ambiguity of many words, the programs had to be allowed to backtrack, look ahead and consult semantic programs in order to arrive at syntactic structurings of sentences. For instance selecting the correct meaning of the word *bank* in *Mary is going to the bank* will become obvious only when it is followed by *in order to get money* or *because she hoped to catch a perch* (note the potential syntactic and semantic ambiguity of the word *perch* which you, as a human language user, probably didn't even notice in the context of that sentence). The trouble is that, once started on this path, where should one stop? If I am standing in a high street when I hear the words *Mary is going to the bank*, I am not likely to assume that Mary is going fishing –

unless I see her coming out of a fishing shop. Even more difficult are cases when semantic content affects decisions about syntactic structures. Two often-quoted sentences are *Time flies like an arrow* and *Fruit flies like a banana*. Deciding about the syntactic relationships depends on knowledge of semantic content. In the first sentence it seems obvious to us, but not to a computer program, that *time* is a noun, *flies* is a verb and *like an arrow* is a descriptive phrase. Despite its word order similarity, the second sentence should be parsed quite differently: the whole phrase *fruit flies* is a noun, *like* is a verb and *a banana* is the object. Correct syntactic analysis requires general knowledge about the differences between an abstract concept like 'time' and examples of living organisms like 'fruit flies'. Difficult as these examples are for a computer program, the fact that they cause no problems for human language understanders demonstrates the ease with which we exploit the meanings of individual words to aid the grammatical structuring of utterances. The relationship between word meanings and the grammatical analysis of sentences is an exceptionally tricky issue for all theories of language understanding.

Language as word meanings

The rules in Chomsky's theory allowed for words to be inserted into syntactic structures after the overall syntactic structure had already been decided on (see Figures 10 and 11). The implication is that syntactic structures can be formulated in isolation from the individual words which make up sentences. It is only after syntactic analysis has been completed and passed on to the semantic component that semantic interpretation of word meanings can begin (see Figure 13). Yet the above examples show that, even during the initial syntactic analysis of a sentence, it obviously makes all the difference which words are included, *time* or *fruit flies*. The presence of the word *can* in *Visiting aunts can be a nuisance* makes it ambiguous whereas *Visiting aunts are a nuisance* can have only one meaning. *The pen in the box* means something quite different from *The box in the pen*, yet they have an identical syntactic structure. It is interesting that, as far as human speakers are concerned, under normal circumstances the only conscious aspect of language use is selecting what words to say. A listener is much more likely to ask 'What does that word mean?' than 'Why have you used a plural verb?' It is only occasionally that adults struggle with getting the grammar right nearly always when they are writing rather than speaking. The 'modern' way of teaching English encourages children to write imaginatively, regardless of grammar, a practice that has led to some disputes between teachers and parents.

This emphasis on word meanings has led to a reversal of the traditional grammar-oriented approach of linguistic theories, notably, of course, Chomsky's transformational grammar. The opposite type of language model is to start with the meanings of words. The argument is that the meaning of an utterance can often be deduced directly from word meanings, relegating grammatical analysis to the subsidiary role of sorting out structural ambiguities if necessary. For most sentences the meaning is obvious from the words; even the scrambled sentence *Flowers the girl by watered are the* would naturally be interpreted as *The flowers are watered by the girl.* In fact it is one test of language ability to be able to unscramble sentences in this way. Even sentences which in isolation are ambiguous are usually uttered in a context which makes the sense quite clear. For instance *The time for Aunt Jane's annual visit is approaching. Visiting aunts can be a nuisance.* In psychological experiments sentences in isolation reveal difficulties with reversible sentences. Syntactic word order has to be taken into account in order to decide between the meanings of *The boy kissed the girl* and *The girl kissed the boy*, although in normal discourse these sentences would only be uttered in some reasonable context, perhaps *Who would have thought she would do it?*

One way of expressing the difference between syntactic theories and those based on word meanings is as follows. Syntactic theories like Chomsky's assume that sentence meanings should be computed on the basis of linguistic rules. In contrast, word meaning theories assume that the meanings of *girls, water, aunts, time, fruit flies* can be directly looked up in a mental lexicon. The advantages and disadvantages of computability versus direct look-up of features was first introduced in Chapter 3 in relation to Collins and Quillian's (1969) semantic hierarchy. It is not easy to decide whether cognitive economy is best served by storing complex linguistic rules, which can be used to generate linguistic structures for whole sets of sentences, or by the potential wastefulness of listing all word meanings in a mental lexicon but facilitating a rapid analysis of semantically obvious sentences by directly looking up word meanings, (see Berwick and Weinberg, 1984).

Schank and his colleagues at Yale developed language understanding computer programs which took as their starting-point the meanings of individual words. Schank (1972) defined word meanings as frames. The primary sense of *give* was defined as a frame with slots for an agent, an act of transferring possession, an object and a recipient. These word definitions are frames in the sense that they define agent, action, object and recipient slots which can be filled in to represent a particular sentence, like *Mary gave the book to John* (see Figure 14). Schank's computer program searched through texts identifying action verbs and then filling in slots with likely agents and objects. These filled-in frames represented the meanings of sentences. For example the sentences *Mary gave the book to John* and *John received a book from Mary* would both be represented as shown in Figure 14. Thus sentence meanings are derived directly from word frames rather than depending on an intial syntactic analysis stage.

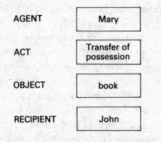

Figure 14 Frame for 'give' sentence.

One problem that word meaning models share with other language understanding theories is the difficulty of deciding on the meanings of words in a single sentence. The frame for *take* may refer to different 'acts' involving transfer of possession, or movement, or the ingestion of a substance, as in *Bill took the book*, *Bill took the train*, *Bill took a pill*. *The bill was large* may refer to the beak of a bird or to an account in a restaurant. Schank fully acknowledges the difficulties of interpreting sentences in isolation. This was in fact the prime motivation for his introduction of the frame-like script and goal representations described in Chapter 4. Scripts are really large-scale frames which incorporate smaller frames for individual actions. The Restaurant script in Figure 8 consists of a sequence of individual actions, like moving to a table, ordering and eating. The verb *enter* would be defined as a 'move' act requiring an agent, *order* as an act requiring a human agent, a 'mental' object and a recipient, *eat* as requiring a 'living' agent and an 'edible' object. The value of setting individual acts within the larger context of a script is that it constrains the possible interpretations of words. The words *give an order* would be taken as referring to giving information about food required, ruling out any other kind of giving, including giving a military order. The interpretation of the 'give' act in *giving a tip* would similarly be confined to a restaurant context.

One of the major issues with theories like Schank's is whether knowledge of the linguistic meanings of words should be separated from general knowledge of the world. It may seem obvious that vocabulary, grammar and semantics are linguistic, while objects, situational contexts and probable events fall within the realm of general knowledge. However, the ability to distinguish between the several possible linguistic meanings of the word *bank* or to identify the syntactic structures of *Time flies like an arrow* and *Fruit flies like a banana* rely on general knowledge about what is likely to occur in the real world. It does seem a trifle uneconomical to have two separate knowledge systems, one a mental lexicon for representing the linguistic meanings of words like *bank*, *time*, *fruit* and *flies*; the other a general knowledge memory store containing semantic hierarchies, schemas and scripts representing real-life objects, such as river banks, financial banks, fruits, bananas, tomatoes and fruit flies, real arrows and metaphorical arrows. What is the linguistic meaning of the word *canary* if it is not that it represents the concept of a bird which has feathers and flies, is yellow and can sing, and is an animal, which means it can move and breathe?

Psychologists who are interested in the levels of letter and word recognition are naturally concerned with the processes by which letter patterns are identified as words, either in isolation or in sentence contexts (see Barber, 1987). But for the purposes of this discussion, it is assumed that, once a word has been recognized, it has access to all the general knowledge associated with that concept.

Schank himself is quite unabashed by the failure to draw a distinction between linguistic and general knowledge. In fact he considers this to be a great strength of his theory of language understanding. He smuggles in a few syntactic ordering rules of the kind needed for recognizing that in a passive sentence the roles of subject and object are changed round. Thus the sentence *A banana is liked by fruit flies* would be mapped on to the frame *Fruit flies* (agent) *like* (action) *a banana* (object). However, to explain why it is unacceptable to say *An arrow is liked by time flies*, there would have to be a frame for 'time', indicating that it is an abstract concept which cannot be an agent. In other words semantic general knowledge dominates the inferential processes required for language understanding. This concern with inferences based on general knowledge has been very influential in psychological theorizing about language use.

Language as knowledge-based inferences

The role of inferences based on general knowledge is particularly important in the comprehension of whole texts and conversations, known as discourse analysis. In the course of putting together the meanings of individual sentences, listeners are constantly making inferences about how they fit together to make a coherent 'story', whether about visiting aunts, singing canaries or an episode in a restaurant. During the 1970s' in reaction to the bitter arguments about the psychological reality of linguistic rules which followed in the wake of the Chomskyan revolution, many psychologists shifted their interests away from syntactic transformations in favour of studying the conditions under which experimental subjects select one interpretation of a story rather than another.

One of the most common research methodologies was to read aloud a list of sentences and then present subjects with a recognition test with a mixture of 'old' sentences, which had been read out, and 'new' sentences, which had never been presented. Subjects had to pick out the sentences which they had just heard. The rationale is that, if subjects confuse 'old' sentences they actually heard with 'new' alternative versions of those sentences, it can be concluded that they must have forgotten the distinctive features which would have distinguished between the two sets of sentences in memory. If people make inferences in order to understand a sentence, these inferences may become so amalgamated into the semantic representation of the sentence that people can no longer recognize the original sentence. Bransford and his colleagues used this recognition confusions method to demonstrate the ubiquity of inferences in understanding. A typical experiment (Bransford, Barclay and Franks, 1972) presented subjects with pairs of sentences, one of which was likely to stimulate an inference while the other was neutral. Examples of such sentences are:

(a) John was trying to fix the bird house and was pounding the nail when his father came out to watch him.
(b) John was trying to fix the bird house and was looking for the nail when his father came out to watch him.

After listening to a list of several sentences, subjects were given a longer list of sentences from which they had to recognize the sentences they had actually heard. As predicted, subjects who had heard sentence (a) were likely to confuse it with the 'new' sentence *John was trying to fix the bird house and was using a hammer when his father came out to watch him*. The explanation was that subjects must have unconsciously made the inference that, if John was pounding a nail, he must have been using a hammer. The subjects who heard sentence (b) had no reason to make an inference that a hammer was being used at just that moment and so were less likely to confuse sentence (b) with the 'new' hammer sentence.

In another type of experiment, reported in Bransford and McCarrell (1975), subjects were presented with sentences that were either easy or difficult to understand.

Easy: The office was cool because the windows were closed.
           The car was moved because he had no change.

Difficult: The trip was not delayed because the bottle shattered.
The haystack was important because the cloth ripped.

In some conditions subjects were given a suitable context for each sentence, for example air conditioning, parking meter, christening a ship, parachuting. With these contextual cues, subjects found it equally easy to make the inferences necessary to understand the difficult sentences as to understand the easy sentences. Finally, an experiment by Bower, Black and Turner (1979) demonstrated that subjects often recall actions which might reasonably be inferred from a script but which had not actually been mentioned, for example that someone had waited in a doctor's waiting-room when this detail had been mentioned only in a story about a dentist's waiting-room.

How are utterances remembered?

It is clear from these experiments that people remember their interpretations of utterances rather than the exact words. The memory representation retains the meaning which has been extracted from an utterance, including any inferences which were involved in comprehending the utterance, for example that John was probably using a hammer. Other experiments have shown that, after hearing a piece of continuous discourse, subjects often confuse the active and passive versions of sentences, thus failing to retain the surface word order of sentences (Sachs, 1967). For instance if they were interrupted while listening to a passage of text, people were unable to decide whether they had heard *He sent a letter about it to Galileo, the great Italian scientist* or other 'new' sentences like *Galileo, the great Italian scientist, was sent a letter about it* or *He sent Galileo, the great Italian scientist, a letter about it*. The subjects in Sachs's experiment were however, easily able to detect changes in meaning, for instance *Galileo, the great Italian scientist, sent a letter to him about it*. In a similar experiment Johnson-Laird and Stevenson (1970) found that subjects confuse sentences with different syntactic deep structures but similar meanings, for example *John liked the painting and he bought it from the duchess* and *The painting pleased John and the duchess sold it to him*. The point here is that *John* is the subject of *liked* but the object of *pleased*. This finding supports Schank's analysis of sentence meanings in terms of underlying actions, according to which *bought* and *sold* would both be examples of an act involving the transfer of objects and money. In an experiment by Bransford and Franks (1971) people did not even notice whether information had been presented as one or more sentences. Given sentences like *The ants were in the kitchen, The jelly was on the table* and *The ants ate the sweet jelly*, people were, if anything, more likely to think that they had heard *The ants in the kitchen ate the sweet jelly which was on the table.*

It may seem obvious that, once people have digested the sense of an utterance, there is no reason why they should remember the syntax or the exact words they heard. Instead they produce a mental representation which updates their model of the world in the light of the new information they have heard. Far from remembering the exact wording of what they hear, people remember only the gist, often a very sketchy gist, as with Bartlett's 'War of the Ghosts' story. It is not surprising that language users are more conscious of meaningful representations than of the largely unconscious and automatic processing stages involved in the extraction of meanings from sentences.

However, this is a good moment to draw attention to the need for some specifically linguistic knowledge. If listeners rely too strongly on inferences based on general knowledge expectations, it might sometimes happen that they simply do not hear what someone is trying to say. They would be in the same position as an observer who is so used to the expected contents of his garden that he is incapable of 'seeing' a panther. There is an extra dimension to linguistic inputs. Since the connection between the sounds *panther* and the meaning of the concept 'panther' is completely arbitrary, language users have to know English before they can respond appropriately to the sounds *There's a panther in your sitting-room*. To a non-speaker of English these sounds would be totally meaningless. What this means is that, even if syntax is not represented as a separate distinctive stage of language understanding, the interaction of words and syntactic word order must in some way be taken into account during language processing. After all, everyone who knows English knows that *The cat sat on the mat* is grammatical and that *Mat the sat cat the on* is not, although general knowledge may suggest the necessary unscrambling of its meaning. The point is that we do not go around talking in cryptically scrambled sentences. The pervasiveness of inferences does not mean that people have the right to churn out gobbledegook just so that we can display our highly developed inferential powers. When two people meet who share no common language, inferences based on mutual knowledge of the situation may give some hints about what each person intends to communicate. But I am sure everyone would agree that this can lead to frustration and misunderstandings which could be rapidly cleared up by knowing how to say in the other person's language, 'Can you tell me the way to the railway station?' or 'Does God exist?' This problem of how to reconcile linguistic knowledge of a language with everyday knowledge of the world is a very real problem. Apart from deliberate attempts to mislead, the aim of speakers and listeners is for linguistic communication to progress as easily as possible. In the next chapter I shall explore some of the assumptions about communicative intentions which are necessary to keep the conversational merry-go-round turning smoothly.

Conclusions

Perhaps I should start by reiterating the point that there are many different, all equally valid, approaches to studying human language. However, it is generally true to say that attempts to express linguistic knowledge solely in terms of syntactic rules have run into the ground, smothered by the complexities of the rules and exceptions of any human language. In his recent writings Chomsky (1981) has distinguished between the 'core' grammar of each language, which is determined by the linguistic universals enshrined in universal grammar, and a periphery of idiosyncratic exceptions which can be learnt only from direct experience of each language. Although Chomsky does not use this terminology, universal grammar can be thought of as a kind of 'frame' which specifies the slots which can be filled in to produce a particular language. Linguistic universals act as parameters which can be allocated particular values. Thus all languages express agents and actions, tenses and moods, but the actual linguistic forms may differ from language to language. According to Chomsky, language learners start with an (innate) knowledge of universal principles which guides their learning of the core grammar of their own native language based on the examples of speech they hear around them. In the absence of any examples to the contrary, a default value, like the most common subject–verb–object order, will be assumed. Any idiosyncratic features, like irregular verbs, will be learnt as a periphery to the main core grammar.

The difficulty is that, whatever universal capabilities are wired into the human brain, one undoubted fact is the diversity of languages which have to be learned. Whether descriptions of language processing are couched in terms of linguistic rules, parsing strategies, word meanings or knowledge-based inferences, the human ability to use the full resources of language to communicate remains a mystery which, even as competent language users ourselves, we cannot explain. One reason for this is the close interpenetration between cognitive abilities and language, as summarized below.

1 In one direction, language influences cognitive processes, the way inputs are interpreted, how information is stored and used. Most of what we mean by intelligent behaviour is judged by people's ability to use language logically and constructively.

2 In the other direction, many kinds of knowledge are necessary for the efficient use of language, notably knowledge of a vocabulary of word meanings, syntactic rules governing word order and inferences based on general knowledge about concepts and probable sequences of events.

3 One issue is whether it is necessary to include a separate syntactic parsing component, or whether sentence representations can be directly generated from word meanings.

4 It has not proved easy to draw a line between the contribution of linguistic knowledge and of general knowledge. In particular, should a mental lexicon of word meanings be distinguished from general knowledge of the concepts to which words refer?

5 Finally, how can the syntactic and semantic processing of sentence meanings be investigated in view of the fact that people remember only the gist of what they read and hear?

6

Language and communication

So far we have been concerned with language understanders operating in isolation, exploiting linguistic knowledge and inferences based on general knowledge, but without having to take into account the intentions of other speakers. The emphasis has been on processing sentences and texts presented by experimenters in order to illuminate the processes necessary for language understanding. But what goes on when speakers attempt to communicate with each other in a real-life setting to win friends and influence other people? Is there anything special about interpreting people's intentions when they use language?

What is communication?

There are many ways in which humans communicate: personal interaction, telephoning, letters, newspaper articles, books, broadcasting, advertisement campaigns, non-verbal gestures, showing off the new car and extravagant clothes. Practically everything people do, even when they are on their own, could be construed as actual or potential communication. The trouble with such a wide definition is that it encompasses all human behaviour. In this chapter I shall be concerned with verbal communication in which words are used in face-to-face situations. There is an account of non-verbal communication and the role of language in defining social status in another volume in this series (Gahagan, 1984).

The use of language to convey meanings in social contexts comes under the heading of pragmatics, so called to distinguish it from syntax and semantics. In the pragmatic arena it is assumed that people already know how to decode utterances into their literal meanings, resolving ambiguities by reference to linguistic contexts. The main question at issue is the selection of appropriate utterances based on mutual understanding of the rules governing conversational interactions.

Language as speech acts

A lot of the impetus in pragmatics has come from philosophers and sociolinguists rather than from psychologists. For many decades sociolinguists have analysed the effects of geography and social class on accents, dialects and speech styles (Trudgill, 1974). They have studied the use of speech in face-to-face situations depending on the social standing of participants, the effect of seating patterns on conversation, and the use of ritual greetings and farewells in situations like parties and railway stations (Argyle, 1973; Goffman, 1971).

Interest in the use of language has also been stimulated by philosophers like Austin (1962) and Searle (1969) who pointed out that speech can be used to perform acts. Some utterances inevitably perform acts: to say *I name you . . .* or *With this ring I thee wed* in itself performs the acts of naming or marriage. These are known as performative utterances because both the form and the content of the act is defined by the words of the utterance. *I pronounce you man and wife* can mean only the act of marriage. Other speech acts indicate the purpose of a communication, for instance whether it is a statement, a request, a question or a command. However, in these cases the actual content of the statement or command has to be formulated as well as using the appropriate speech act. Thus *Close the window* and *Open the window* both have the form of a 'command' speech act but their semantic meaning is diametrically opposed. Moreover, as Searle pointed out, many communicative acts are achieved by the use of indirect speech acts. Although the utterance *I'm cold* is in the form of a 'statement' speech act, it can also be intended as a 'request' speech act aimed at getting someone to shut the window, rather than as a simple statement about the speaker's temperature.

A question which immediately comes to mind is how listeners know when to interpret an utterance as signifying one speech act rather than another. Why is *I'm cold* sometimes interpreted as a plain statement, sometimes as a request, sometimes as a complaint? In what circumstances might *Mind you, I don't promise anything* be taken as an implicit indirect promise, despite the apparently contradictory words selected. The implication is that the listener has to rely on some other information over and above the literal content of an utterance in order to discover what the speaker intended to say. What is required is some way of relating speech acts to contexts in which they make sense.

One of Searle's important contributions was to outline the contextual conditions necessary for the interpretation of speech acts. For instance making a request depends on the speaker wishing to change the situation and the listener being in a position to do something about it. So, faced with the utterance of the words *I'm cold*, the listener has to work out whether the situation conforms to Searle's 'felicity' conditions for a request. If the listener believes that the speaker likes being cold, and/or there is no feasible action the listener can take to alter the situation, the 'request' meaning will fail. The listener will then have to consider other speech act interpretations of *I'm cold*. For instance if someone had just asked the speaker how he felt, this might incline the listener to act on the assumption that the speaker's intended speech act was to make a statement. This analysis of speech acts raises the difficult question of the relation between the literal meaning of an utterance and its intended meaning. Does it even make sense to talk about the literal meaning of *I'm cold* if it can 'mean' so many different speech acts. According to speech act theory, conversational responses are determined by interpretations of intended speech acts rather than by the literal meaning of an utterance.

In the same vein the philosopher Grice (1975) stated certain co-operative principles which govern intelligible conversations. Grice's co-operative principles include maxims like:

Quality: say only what you know to be true
Quantity: provide no more and no less information than is required
Relation: be relevant
Manner: be brief and avoid ambiguity.

Of course, these are ideals which it is unlikely that most conversations will achieve. There are occasions when the object of a conversation is to pass the time of day or to enjoy a spicy piece of gossip or to flatter someone outrageously. The basic idea, though, is that there is an implicit contract between the participants in a conversation about the purpose of communications.

Bridging inferences and audience design

Clark is a psychologist who took seriously the notion that there is a contract between speaker and hearer. Clark (1977) suggested that the listener is entitled to assume that a speaker is trying to convey a coherent message about a specific given topic. A good conversationalist makes sure that a listener has, or can reasonably be expected to infer, any required information about the topic under discussion. Remarks which introduce a new topic are often prefaced by statements like *You know the old house we saw last week*. Sometimes the topic is obvious, particularly between close friends. Writing a letter to a friend is very different from writing for an unknown audience of readers. Skilled writers take care to remove potential ambiguities in their prose, avoiding sentence constructions which could be interpreted in more than one way. Sometimes things go wrong in spite of every effort. A nice example is given by Parsons (1969):

> Completing an impressive ceremony, the Admiral's lovely daughter smashed a bottle over her stern as she slid gracefully down the slipways.

Because of our tendency to make inferences about the situation being described, the writer – and probably many of his readers –

simply didn't notice the ambiguity of the possible references for the pronouns 'her' and 'she'.

Chapter 5 stressed the importance of inferences and expectations in achieving coherent interpretations of discourse, whether in the form of conversations or written texts. If listeners were incapable of inferring that someone who is pounding a nail is likely to be using a hammer, they would not be able to make head or tail of sentences like *John was pounding a nail. He shouted 'ouch' as the hammer hit his finger.* Whether or not a listener had already made the inference that John was pounding the nail with a hammer, the inference must be available in order to understand the next sentence about the hammer hitting his finger. Clark (1977) called these kinds of inferences 'bridging inferences' because they are needed to bridge the gaps between consecutive sentences in a discourse. In particular he thought they were necessary to establish the 'given' topic of a conversational exchange, as opposed to any 'new' information a speaker might wish to convey.

Clark went on to make the point that listeners can understand sentences only if they already have in mind a given topic to which they can attach any new information. If the topic is not obviously stated, the listener is bound by the speaker/listener contract to make a bridging inference to decide what the topic must be. For instance it would be the listener's duty to make the bridging inference that the hammer which hit John's finger was the same hammer he was pounding the nail with. In other words, it must be assumed that the 'hammer' is the topic referred to and, for that matter, that the pronouns *he* and *his* in the second sentence refer back to John. Another example is that listeners will be able to understand the sentence *She left to go home* only if they can allocate a reference for 'she'. They may identify Sue as the topic of *She left to go home* by making the inference that the speaker must be referring to someone already known or recently mentioned. Or they may have to make a bridging inference from a prior statement like *Sue was looking ill. She left to go home.* Even without knowing who Sue is, it is obvious that the speaker intended the listener to assume that the two remarks *Sue was looking ill* and *She left to go home* are intended to refer to the same topic as part of a coherent discourse.

Clark and his colleagues carried out experiments to test the notion of bridging inferences. In one such experiment (Haviland and Clark, 1974) subjects were presented with pairs of sentences and had to press a button when they felt they had understood each sentence. An example of a sentence pair is:

(a) George got some beer out of the car. The beer was warm.
(b) Andrew was especially fond of beer. The beer was warm.

The contrast was between reaction times to the second sentence *The beer was warm* depending on whether a bridging inference needed to be made from the first sentence. As predicted, subjects responded faster to the second sentence in (a) because there is a *direct* reference in the first sentence to the *beer* which is the topic of the second sentence. In (b) the reference in the first sentence is to *beer* in general, thus requiring subjects to make a bridging inference that the topic of the second sentence is some of his favourite beer which Andrew must have brought to the picnic, which was – by American standards – too warm. The assumption is that bridging inferences take extra time, at least in the context of a psychology experiment.

Bridging inferences depend on general knowledge based on past experiences of the world. If we don't know that the word *beer* refers to a drink, the sentences might seem rather mysterious. Lack of knowledge about the rituals involved in launching ships would make the Parson's quote decidedly odd. The point has been made in previous chapters that general knowledge is vital in interpreting all inputs from the environment. However, there is an added ingredient when language is involved. Interactions with the physical environment can be thought of as a matter between an individual and his immediate context. Communication depends on an appreciation of other people's intentions. Inferences in the context of language are motivated by the belief that the speaker or writer *intended* us to make that inference. If I see some beer being taken out of a car, I may or may not make any inferences. But if I am engaged in conversation with someone, then it is essential that I make any obviously intended inferences if I want to continue the conversation. If a listener continually interrupts by saying *What beer?*, *Who is Sue?*, *What do you mean by saying you are cold?* conversation would soon come to a complete standstill. Listeners make bridging inferences on the assumption that a speaker must have meant them to make such an inference. In return, the speaker is bound to ensure that the listener could reasonably be expected to make any necessary inferences. In order to adhere to the principles of the speaker/ listener contract, a speaker who says *I walked into a fairyland of lights* should do so only if the external context, or the topic of the previous conversation, makes it clear whether a listener should take this as referring to a fairy story, a dance or a seaside pier.

Clark and Murphy (1982) conceptualized this mutual under- standing between speakers and hearers as the principle of 'audience design'. By this they meant that speakers design their utterances to achieve relevance to a particular audience at a particular time. Listeners act on the assumption that speakers have tailored their speech to their particular requirements and so they interpret utterances in the light of any conclusions speakers must have intended them to draw. One of Clark and Murphy's examples is Anne saying to Pierre *Look at that man*. If there is a man and a woman walking by it is obvious to whom she is referring. But even if there are two men, Pierre will work on the assumption that there is something so obviously bizarre about one of them that Anne didn't think it necessary to indicate which man she meant. Two other examples quoted by Clark, *The photographer asked the man to do a Napolean for the camera* and *My sister managed to Houdini her way into her office this morning* make perfect sense as long as you know who Napoleon and Houdini were. It would be a failure of audience design to use such expressions if the speaker suspects that the listener does not share the speaker's knowledge about who Houdini was, or for that matter if the speaker's sister has never been mentioned before. On the other hand, only the most literal-minded and annoying listener would complain that *I saw a Picasso today, I bought a bed clock, This ballet book is interesting* should really be expressed as *I saw a picture by Picasso, I bought a clock to put beside my bed, This book about ballet is interesting*.

The implication of this approach is that the literal meanings of utterances communicate very little unless spoken in a particular context of mutual knowledge. It is only when a speaker and listener know that their shared knowledge is mutual that communication is successful. However, one danger about the insistence on complete mutual knowledge is that a speaker and listener can get locked into an infinite regress of inferences. If a speaker says something puzzling, the listener is supposed to assume that the speaker intends to refer to some mutually shared knowledge. If nothing comes to mind immediately, the listener has to assume that there must be some shared meaning that the speaker was assuming that the listener should assume. For example if I say *'That's a nice house'*, theoretically I should be in a position of knowing that my listener knows which house I am refering to, and that she knows that I know she knows, and that I know that she knows that I know she knows, and so on *ad infinitum*. The point is that in principle there is no limit to the number of assumptions which might be necessary in order to ensure that speaker and hearer share exactly the same knowledge about each other's state of knowledge.

Language should be relevant

Sperber and Wilson (1986) cast doubt on the need to establish fully shared mutual knowledge. Certainly it is necessary for speaker and listener to assume communicative intentions. However, in order to avoid an infinity of inferences, Sperber and Wilson suggest that participants in a conversation do not aim at absolutely fail-safe communication. Instead they limit the assumptions which need to be made to those which add some useful contextual information in order to interpret an utterance. Sperber and Wilson's definition of relevance is that an assumption (that is a bridging inference) is relevant only if it has large contextual effects *and* requires relatively little processing effort. They give as an example the following exchange (which they say they really overheard although it sounds as if it might have come straight from a play by Harold Pinter):

Flag-seller: 'Would you like to buy a flag for the Royal National Lifeboat Institution?'
Passer-by: 'No thanks. I always spend my holidays with my sister in Birmingham.'

To understand the passer-by's answer the hearer has to make quite a lot of inferences. The point is that assumptions that the passer-by will never need a lifeboat because he never goes on holiday to the seaside are justified because they guarantee a successful context for understanding. Incidentally what made me assume that the passer-by is a man, and probably lives on his own? These assumptions imply that minimal further bridging inferences would be needed to comprehend a continuation of the conversation along the following lines:

Flag-seller: 'What about your children then?'
Passer-by: 'Their mother lives in Rugby.'

Sperber and Wilson's theory assumes that people adhere to the principle of optimal relevance. Optimal relevance is achieved when necessary inferences are sufficiently relevant to warrant extra processing effort. Normally the speaker or writer provides a context which makes it obvious what he or she is trying to communicate. Even a cryptic comment like *John's if he gets here in time* is a perfectly comprehensible reply to *Whose father is giving Mary a lift*? Sometimes communicators, for example writers of difficult textbooks, may believe that they are adhering to the principle of relevance when the amount of processing required is too onerous for readers to grasp the remote assumptions taken for granted by the writer.

Sperber and Wilson also cite the case of bores who produce monologues which are of no relevance to their audiences. Such speakers certainly contravene Grice's maxim to provide no more information than is required. However, these communications do not necessarily break the optimal relevance principle because comprehending their intended meanings may require very little processing effort. As defined by Sperber and Wilson, predictable utterances are relevant since relatively few assumptions have to be processed in order to recognize what the speaker intends to say. It is harder to explain why readers often rate extra processing effort well worthwhile to unravel the intricate plotting of a detective story or the nuances of a complex but fascinating novel, even if the full meaning of what the author intended to communicate remains somewhat obscure. Sperber and Wilson have a tendency to confound the interest value of a communication with the technical definition of relevance. Optimal relevance implies that communications are most relevant when their intentions are transparent and require little processing, a recipe you might think for a boring and unsurprising conversationalist.

Language as commitments

Both Clark (1977) and Sperber and Wilson (1986) take the line that conversations depend on a contract between speakers and hearers to achieve relevant interpretations. Winograd and Flores (1986) took up the idea that communications can be understood only as a pattern of commitments by participants. It is interesting to note that in the 1970s Winograd (1972) had introduced his well-known language-understanding computer program called SHRDLU, which interpreted typed-in linguistic inputs about a small world of toy blocks. This had been part of the enterprise of creating 'artificial intelligence' language-understanding computer programs. Although Winograd's syntactic component was allowed to call in information about word meanings from a semantic component, and about the positioning of the toy blocks from a knowledge component, the aim of the program was to parse sentences into explicit instructions and statements. Later Winograd (1980) drew attention to the drawbacks of his earlier assumption that utterances can be decoded into literal meanings. Like others, he demonstrated that utterances, rather than representing literal meanings in the minds of speakers and hearers, can be interpreted quite differently depending on speakers' and hearers' intentions and knowledge.

In their book Winograd and Flores (1986) widened the stage to look at the overall structure of whole conversations rather than concentrating on the understanding of individual utterances. They suggest that a conversation should be thought of as a 'dance' in which speech acts follow one another in a 'mutual coupling' between language users. After each commitment to a speech act by a speaker, for example to make a request, there are various options for the other participant, such as to promise to carry out the request, reject it or to make a counter request. In turn, the first participant can accept, withdraw, and so on. Possible moves and countermoves after an initial request by A are shown in Figure 15. At state 2 the arrows show that B can promise to comply with A's request, moving on to state 3. Other alternatives for B are to reject the request or to enter into negotiations by producing a counter-offer, for example *I will go to the shops but only if you give me some money to buy an ice-cream.* Depending on which state B reaches, A has different possibilities

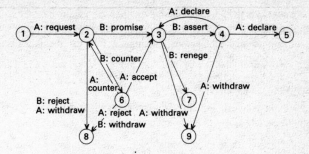

Figure 15 A conversational 'dance'.
Source: Winograd and Flores (1986).

for reply, by withdrawing the request, continuing negotiations with counter-offers, and so on.

The point Winograd and Flores are making is that conversations are carried on against a background of joint social purposes. If people ignore implicit commitments, communication will break down and may leave a residue of mistrust which will affect future social interactions. Winograd (1980) gives several examples of what happens when a speaker ignores the implicit commitments of a speech act and so confuses potential listeners. One of Winograd's examples is the oddity, indeed the bad faith, of a speaker using the statement *Joan has never failed a student in her linguistics class* to express the fact that Joan has never taught a linguistics class. It is strictly possible that one reason why Joan has never failed any students is that she never took the class at all. But the normal interpretation would be that the 'given' topic is that Joan certainly *had* taught a linguistics class and that the 'new' information is that she never failed a student. Another of Winograd's examples demonstrates that even a simple word like *water* has no single literal meaning but is open to different interpretations, depending on the conversation in which it is embedded.

A: 'Is there any water in the fridge?'
B: 'Yes.'
A: 'Where? I don't see it.'
B: 'In the cells of the tomato.'

In a case like this, A would be entitled to claim that B's first response ignored the obvious implications of his request for something to drink. Between intimates the situation might be saved by assuming that a joke was intended. Another example of 'bad faith' by ignoring a speaker's obviously intended speech act is typical of schoolboy humour.

A: 'Can you tell me the time?'
B: 'Yes.'

The emphasis on speech acts, speakers' intentions and listeners' knowledge adds richness to our understanding of language use. The only proviso is that all these approaches assume that people already know how to speak a particular language. In the above conversational exchanges, speaker A would have been even more taken aback if B had replied volubly in a foreign language A was not familiar with. Although the word *water* can mean lots of things, it is unlikely to be used to refer to a zebra, although I suppose there is water in the cells of a zebra. The point is that words do have an agreed range of possible meanings. Although it may well be impossible to define all the possible uses of a word in advance, it is our knowledge of the English word *water* that makes us smile at the 'water in the fridge' example. In another language different words might be used for 'drinkable water' and for the 'water content in cells' which would have prevented the confusion. This is what makes jokes in one language so difficult to translate into another language. A well-known but probably apochryphal story is the translation into Russian of *The spirit is willing but the flesh is weak* as something along the lines of *The vodka is flowing but the steak is tired*.

Conclusions

The relationship between the literal linguistic meanings of utterances, on the one hand, and general knowledge about speakers' intentions and conversational relevance, on the other, remains the great puzzle of human communication. However, part of the controversy between those who emphasize the linguistic nature of language understanding and these who emphasize the role of general knowledge simply comes down to how 'understanding' is defined. Researchers who are interested in communication define understanding as appreciating all the nuances of intended meanings, whether an utterance is intended as a statement, a serious enquiry or an ironic joke. Researchers who stress the importance of linguistic relationships define understanding as extracting the syntactic structures necessary for understanding the meaning of an utterance. Fodor (1983) defines the 'shallow' output of the linguistic input system as being 'what is said' as opposed to 'what is meant', thus ruling out speculations about speakers' intentions. The problem is to decide whether 'what is said' refers only to recognizing the words in an utterance or whether it also includes extracting the literal meaning of a sentence. Fodor hovers between these two definitions. This is because it is so difficult to draw a clear distinction between the precise literal meaning of 'what is said' and the shades of interpretation that depend on 'what is meant'. The literal meaning of *Can you tell me the time?* is indeed a question about someone's ability, equivalent to *Can you drive a car?* Yet English speakers are virtually certain to interpret the first question as a speech act requesting information about the time, rather than as asking a simple question, to be answered 'yes' or 'no'. The only basis for this assumption seems to be general knowledge about 'time' as a type of information, which incidentally can 'fly like an arrow'.

In one sense of understanding, we must be able to recognize words and appreciate possible syntactic combinations of words. In the conversation about water in the fridge the speakers could 'hear' and 'understand' each others' words and sentences, even though they may have been baffled by the selection of these particular utterances in that particular context. In another context, like a textbook, referring to the water in the cells of the tomato would be entirely appropriate. To understand the significance of even a simple sentence like *The cat sat on the mat*, we have to know whether it appears in a children's reading book or as an example in a book about linguistics. Another rather nice example I came across recently is the advertising slogan *Foiled again? Come to Dillons Bookshop*. It is a moot point whether the literal meaning for the vocabulary item *foiled* will have been appreciated in its full richness if the reader doesn't know that Foyles is *the* great rival to Dillons among the academic bookshops in London.

The inferences required to interpret linguistic inputs can be thought of as exploiting exactly the same general knowledge as is needed to interpret all other objects and events in the environment. But there are two kinds of knowledge which do seem to be special to language communications. The first is linguistic knowledge which, difficult as it may be to describe, constitutes the difference between knowing how to speak a language and not being able to speak a language. Secondly, participation in linguistic interchanges requires knowledge of other people's intentions to communicate. The selection of spoken and written utterances has to be geared to the mutual knowledge of participants. This means that, in addition to the questions raised at the end of the previous chapter in relation to language use in general, there are important extra considerations which rely on language users' communicative intentions. This has raised some extremely important issues which are listed below.

1 A very influential notion has been to think of utterances as speech acts which perform various conversational functions.
2 Speakers and listeners are bound by a contract which constrains speakers to provide sufficient contextual information and listeners to make inferences based on what speakers obviously expect them to know.
3 Context is an important factor in deciding which of the many possible bridging inferences are relevant to a particular exchange of speech acts.
4 It is not easy to reconcile linguistic knowledge of literal meanings, which constitutes knowing how to speak a language, with the wide range of possible interpretations depending on speakers' and listeners' commitments in a communicative context.

7

Knowledge, speech and action: the halfway mark

It may be useful to sum up where we have got to so far. What I have called passive knowledge refers to a permanent long-term repository of mental representations which constitutes a record of past experiences of the world. Knowledge may take the form of conceptual semantic knowledge which has been abstracted from many similar experiences of objects and events; it may take the form of personal memories, including autobiographical facts and autobiographical events; it may take the form of rules and procedures for producing and interpreting language.

All this can be thought of as a store of knowledge which people carry around with them for dealing with the objects and events encountered in daily life. Each new input from the environment stimulates the retrieval of relevant knowledge into active working memory. Mostly this will occur as an automatic reminding process of some incident in the past; sometimes as the result of a conscious memory search to locate some useful fact or similar past experience. Either way, on the basis of the current contents of active memory, new experiences will be interpreted.

These interpretations take the form of new mental representations of the environment. These new representations may activate further information, including procedures for generating a suitable response. Finally, the new representations, and the consequences of any responses, may be merged into permanent knowledge as useful updates of our mental model of the environment. Temporary representations of inputs, such as the exact words in a sentence, or the details of a particular episode, may be forgotten as soon as the new information is absorbed into general knowledge.

The message of all this is that knowledge is designed to be used. For this to happen, knowledge representations must be organized in such a way that relevant memories can easily be retrieved. This was the motivation behind the models of memory discussed in Chapters 3 and 4. The main conclusion reached in those chapters was that knowledge is organized in a variety of ways depending on the method by which that knowledge is tested. If people are asked to judge whether canaries are birds, they are able to access a hierarchy of concepts. If they are asked to produce the typical features of a dog or a table, they can do that too. It was argued in Chapter 4 that schemas, represented as frames, appear to offer the most plausible organization of knowledge for interpreting new events and language inputs. Frame representations for word meanings and script frames for expected sequences of actions have the advantage of providing knowledge frameworks for interpreting naturally occurring events.

There were four major drawbacks, however, in implementing schema models.

1 Most reminding of similar past events is automatic and so not accessible to consciousness.
2 The possible inferences that can be made about situations are so numerous that it is difficult to pin them down in a psychological theory.
3 General semantic knowledge has to be adapted to cope with interpretations of idiosyncratic individual events.
4 How do people know when it is sensible to update their permanent general knowledge as opposed to noting an event or action as a one-off occurrence?

In Chapters 5 and 6 the same kinds of knowledge relationships were discussed in relation to language. There are, however, several important differences between language and other spheres of experience. Perhaps they all hang on the one crucial fact that language is at one remove from experience. If you actually *see* John pounding a nail with his shoe, you may be reminded of a hammer but you will not allow yourself to infer that what you are actually seeing *is* a hammer. You may be predisposed to seeing panthers in zoos but, however surprising it might be, you would have to admit to the reality of seeing a panther in your garden. The great advantage of language is that it can be used to describe all sorts of unreal possibilities, to discuss alternative plans and to carry us along in great flights of artistic imagination. On the other hand, stereotypes introduced by language are often responsible for us 'seeing' what we expect to see; for instance 'all redheads have fiery tempers'. Both the advantages and disadvantages of language being at one remove from reality stem from its arbitrary symbolic nature. It is often said that it doesn't matter whether I 'see' a colour differently from someone else as long as we both call it *red*. Speakers of a language have to agree on linguistic conventions, even if they sometimes use them to convey different thoughts. Another feature of linguistic knowledge is that it forms part of our most permanent knowledge. Apart from learning the meanings of new words, or adopting a fashionable buzz word or phrase, linguistic knowledge has to be impervious to the idiosyncracies of particular utterances. Otherwise, knowledge of a language would be continually shifting, ending up with a community of native speakers who can no longer understand each other.

In all social interactions people have to take into account the motivations of other people with whom they come in contact. One will not get very far in life without the ability to 'read' other people's minds and intentions from their behaviour towards ourselves. But in the case of speech there is the extra dimension of a contract between speaker and hearer to fulfil the conventions required for successful communication. A speaker is expected to provide the background knowledge necessary for understanding the topic and the listener is expected to make inferences on the assumption that the speaker intends the communication to make sense. Because of the symbolic nature of language, these conventions extend to irony, sarcasm and gossip as well as to plain statements of information that *canaries can sing* and that *the beer is warm*, which are the staples of psychological research.

Of course, speech is a type of action, indeed one of the most typical of human actions. But language is still often thought of as coming within the realm of intellectual abilities. Humans are knowing, thinking and talking animals but they are also capable of physical actions. The question I shall be considering in the remaining chapters is how people learn to act. In other words, what turns a man of thought into a man of action? What accounts for the ability to trade on relevant past experiences when planning new actions? If an analogy is spotted between past and present, a strategy which has proved successful in the past can be brushed off for use again. How and when are creative adaptations implemented and novel solutions reabsorbed into old knowledge? Are there general problem-solving strategies which apply across the board or do problem-solving skills emerge out of expert knowledge of a specific domain? Is there such a thing as a generally expert 'thinker' or is an expert simply someone who has learnt a lot of specific skills? Is it really true that 'the more we know, the less we have to think'? The influence of old knowledge on solving new problems will be the topic of the next chapter.

Problem-solving

In one sense everything I have talked about so far can be thought of as problem-solving. Deciding how to categorize and respond to an object poses a problem. If there really is a panther in the garden something has to be done about it pretty quickly. Reading books and talking to people involve problems of interpretation. It is true that IQ tests and logical puzzles are the problems most commonly used in psychological research. But in a wider sense it could be claimed that humans are never stirred into action unless they are faced with a problem of some kind.

What is problem-solving?

Problems have been defined as arising whenever a path to a desired goal is blocked, literally in the case of rats running down mazes. 'Any action taken by a person in pursuit of a blocked goal, whether physical or mental, is regarded as problem solving' is the definition given by Kahney (1986). On the face of it this sounds like a suitably general characterization of all problem-solving activities. A bus that breaks down, a letter turning down an application, a tennis match coming up, all these are 'blocks' which have to be dealt with by some sort of strategic action to achieve the desired goal. Sometimes the goal itself may have to be changed in some way but even this requires some active problem-solving behaviour. However, it is not as easy as it sounds for psychologists to study problem-solving. In fact I am not really being too unkind if I emphasize the major differences between problem-solving as investigated in psychological experiments and the kinds of problems which have to be solved in real life. For one thing, many everyday problems are solved so quickly that they don't even appear to be problems. If I find I haven't got enough change to put in a ticket machine my goal of getting a ticket is blocked. But I have well-rehearsed strategies for asking someone for change or, if the worst comes to the worst, standing in line at the ticket office.

In order to avoid routine problem-solving, psychologists tend to use tasks which are sufficiently puzzling to stimulate people into displaying active and sustained problem-solving behaviour, giving experimenters some behaviour to observe and measure. It is particularly desirable if a problem continues to require thought even after a solution has first been discovered. This is in contrast to problems like the Duncker radiation problem or the nine dot problem; once the solution is known, the entire mystery is exploded. A further requirement for psychological research is that the answers to problems should be well defined. This is a necessary precondition for deciding when a solver has reached a correct solution. But it tends to rule out the open-ended 'creative' types of problem-solving which are more common in real life, such as how do I go about getting promotion? Another aim of psychological research has been to study 'pure' problem-solving, uncontaminated by previous experience. The puzzles presented to subjects in psychological experiments are selected in the hope that they will be novel. As we shall see later, it is a vain hope to study any human activity without taking into account prior experience and knowledge.

Finally, the whole point of thought is that people do not spring into action but engage in thinking before they act. I pointed out in Chapter 2 that one of the great advantages of thought is that strategies can be tried out in the mind before a full commitment to action. But how can psychologists 'externalize' the thinking processes which lead to the selection of one problem-solving strategy rather than another? The major methodology is that originally adopted by Duncker of getting subjects to talk aloud while solving a problem. Nowadays, of course, these talking aloud verbal protocols have escalated with the introduction of tape recorders. Recordings of problem-solvers' speech are taken as evidence of the way people represent problems to themselves and the twists and turns that lead them towards a solution. Despite criticisms that talking aloud may distort normal thinking, and inevitably ignores the unconscious processes which lead to sudden insights (Nisbett and Wilson, 1977), reliance on verbal protocols is the most common method for observing problem-solving in action, despite all the stops and starts, 'ums' and 'ahs'.

Computer models of problem-solving

Another way of 'externalizing' problem-solving strategies is to write computer programs which ape human problem-solving abilities. The argument is that both computers and human problem-solvers are information processing machines. In both cases information about a problem is input and internally represented. Various computations are carried out in order to produce a sequence of actions. Simon (1979) and others have suggested that, because of this essential similarity between humans and computers as processors of information, it is possible to compare the representation of a problem in the database of a computer with that of a human solver. To take an example, suppose that both a human and a computer are presented with the well-known Tower of Hanoi pegs and rings puzzle. The starting position for this problem is shown in Figure 16. The goal is to get all the rings from peg A over to peg C in the same order from biggest ring to smallest ring. In case this seems much too easy, the rules state that only one ring can be moved at a time and that at no time can a bigger ring be placed on top of a smaller ring. If you try this out in your mind's eye, or by drawing out some 'pegs' and 'rings', you will probably find that you will take several goes before achieving an efficient way of arriving at the solution.

If a computer program is presented with this problem, the

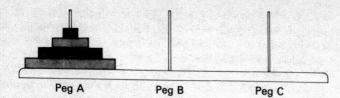

Peg A   Peg B   Peg C

Figure 16 Tower of Hanoi problem.
Moving one ring at a time, and one ring only, try to move the
configuration of four rings over to the far right-hand peg, so that the
rings end up in the same order (biggest on the bottom, etc.) *You may not
place any ring on top of a smaller ring*. And, of course, rings may only be
placed on one of the three pegs, not placed elsewhere on the table.

programmer has to include specific instructions which will allow
the computer to 'move' rings from one peg to another. The
rationale is that the 'moves' made by the computer program can
be compared with those made by a human problem-solver.
There may, of course, be revealing differences between the
'artificial intelligence' displayed by the computer as compared
with human 'natural intelligence'. In fact one of the main uses of
verbal protocols is to see whether the instructions incorporated
into a computer program succeed in simulating the problem-
solving processes revealed by what a person says he thinks he is
doing.

Within an information processing framework Simon (1979)
has characterized problem-solving as requiring an interaction
between an information processing system (the problem-solver
– whether human or machine), a task environment (the rules
of the problem) and a problem space. The problem space
is the problem-solver's own internal representation of the
task environment. In humans, more often than not, the
representation of a problem space reflects only a partial
understanding of the formal structure of a problem. Newell and
Simon (1972) report one of the first attempts to program a
computer to 'think'. Their program was known as the General
Problem Solver (GPS). The GPS was designed to model the
inferences necessary to prove geometry theorems and was later
extended to other logical problems. It might seem that making
the logical deductions necessary to prove a theorem in geometry

would be a straightforward matter of applying a set of mathematical rules, just the kind of thing computers are good at. But the difficulty is that there are many, many deductions that can be made at any point in a proof, only a few of which are relevant to the particular theorem being proved. Humans learning geometry have to use their judgement about which steps are likely to prove a theorem. In order to carry out this selection process, it proved necessary to incorporate heuristic strategies into the GPS program which would help it to select from all possible logical steps only those which were relevant to achieving the goal of proving a particular theorem. These strategies are called 'heuristic' or 'rule of thumb' strategies in contrast to algorithms. Algorithms are rules which automatically achieve a solution, for example the rules for long division. Heuristics are guidelines for selecting actions that are most likely to lead a solver towards a goal, but may not always do so.

Means ends analysis

As explained by Simon (1979), one general heuristic strategy is to incorporate progress tests which indicate whether a solver is 'getting warmer' in the sense of getting nearer to the goal. This was formulated in GPS and later computer programs as means ends analysis. It is called this because it is concerned with selecting a 'means' which will achieve an 'end', leading to a goal solution. The essence of means ends analysis is that it selects operations which will reduce the distance between the current situation and the current goal. For example in a program for solving geometry theorems, at each point the program selects a method, carries out certain deductions, and then tests to see whether these have succeeded in narrowing the distance towards the current goal. Depending on the outcome of this test, the program either moves on to the next step, tries another method, or gives up altogether. The major aim of an heuristic is to reduce a problem to manageable proportions by increasing the selectivity of the program in choosing which operations to carry out. The means ends heuristic provides a method for evaluating the relevance of actions according to whether they are useful in achieving a current goal.

Often it is not possible to achieve the main goal all in one step.

So another important characteristic of means ends analysis is to break down the main goal into subgoals. This amounts to analysing a problem into subproblems, each of which has to be solved before the final goal can be reached. A real life situation which is amenable to means ends analysis is a travel plan (Kahney, 1986). For instance the actions needed to transport 'me at home' to 'me in Trafalgar Square' might be selected by evaluating whether they help to decrease the distance between me and my goal, which is Trafalgar Square. It may be necessary to set up a subgoal of transporting 'me at home' to 'me at Milton Keynes station' which might lead to the action 'take a taxi to Milton Keynes station'. Although it seems natural to choose examples of means ends analysis in which distance to a goal can be literally measured in kilometres, it is important to note that distance from a goal or subgoal need not be taken so literally. A necessary subgoal might be to pack a suitcase. What is required is a measure which reflects the distance to this goal. In this case this would be defined as a specific number of travel needs which have to be packed into the suitcase. If a toothbrush is missing, a new subgoal will have to be set up of obtaining a toothbrush. Operations would then be evaluated according to whether they reduce the distance between the present state and this new subgoal, for example looking for the toothbrush or buying a new one, which in turn would set up a new subgoal of going to the shops. A typical goal and subgoal structure for means ends analysis is shown in Figure 17.

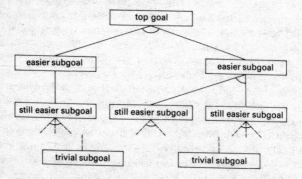

Figure 17 Means ends analysis into goals and subgoals.

Problem-solving computer programs using means ends analysis have had some success in simulating the verbal protocols of subjects when they are solving problems for which there is a reasonably clear goal and subgoal structure. For instance the Tower of Hanoi puzzle can be analysed as a set of interlocking subgoals for moving the largest ring to peg C, then the next largest, and so on. Unfortunately, despite the obvious appeal of means ends analysis as a heuristic strategy for evaluating progress towards a goal, humans are often unable to look ahead sufficiently to grasp the overall goal structure of a problem. This means that they have no basis for evaluating progress towards subgoals and goals. Many puzzles are selected for experiments precisely because the basis for selecting the shortest path of moves to reach the final goal is not at all obvious. One example is the Missionaries and Cannibals problem, in which three missionaries and three cannibals have to be transported by boat across a river without allowing the number of cannibals to outnumber the number of missionaries on either bank, in which case the cannibals will put the missionaries in the pot (see Figure 18). In a problem like this, the final goal is clear enough but the subgoals required to achieve a solution are much less clear. Progress cannot be measured simply by the total number of people transported from the left bank to the right bank; if there are too many cannibals on the right bank, the missionaries will get eaten.

It is possible to work out a sequence of all possible moves for transporting the missionaries and cannibals across the river and to plot the quickest path of moves towards a solution. In fact it is not a particularly hard problem for a computer to solve. This makes it all the more interesting that human problem-solvers cannot hold this type of structure in their limited capacity working memories. Polson and his colleagues have studied waterjug problems, which involve pouring quantities of water between jugs of different sizes in order to end up with a specified volume of water (see Figure 19). As Atwood and Polson (1976) point out, it is not easy to break down a waterjug problem into subgoals. This is because the selection of pouring-water 'moves' is determined by how they contribute to the final goal. Atwood, Masson and Polson (1980) demonstrated that, even when subjects were given information at each stage about all possible

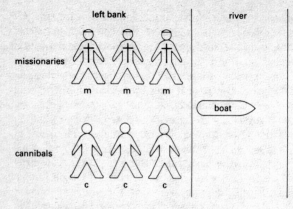

Figure 18 Missionaries and cannibals problem.
Three missionaries and three cannibals seek to cross a river from the left bank to the right bank. A boat is available which will hold two people and which can be navigated by any combination of missionaries and cannibals involving not more than two and not less than one person. If the missionaries on either bank of the river are outnumbered at any time by cannibals, the cannibals will indulge their anthropophagic tendencies and eat the missionaries. When the boat is moored at a bank, its passengers are regarded as being on that bank.

moves for pouring water from one jug to another, they were still unable to plan a sequence of moves based on a means ends analysis of the whole problem which would get them from the initial state to the goal state. Subjects were given this information on a computer screen and they were able to press buttons to make 'pouring' moves and to erase any undesirable or illegal moves. Nevertheless, they simply could not keep track in active working memory of an overall plan for carrying out a whole sequence of moves; nor of the consequences of the varying amounts of water in each jug after several moves of pouring water from one jug into another. In order to simulate the behaviour of human solvers, Polson and his colleagues developed a computer program which selected moves in waterjug problems by gradually learning to avoid repeating unsuccessful moves. The computer was given an artificial limit on the number of previous moves which could be remembered in short-term working memory. With these limitations the program was successful in simulating the gradual improvement in performance of human problem-solvers (Atwood and Polson, 1976). It was only very gradually that solvers learned to avoid moves that lead them back to previously unsuccessful states. Polson and his colleagues believe that people are capable of only limited means ends analysis subject to working memory constraints.

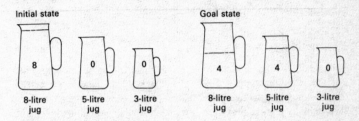

Figure 19 A waterjug problem.
The aim is to move from the initial state of 8 litres in the biggest jug to the goal state of 4 litres in each of the biggest and second biggest jugs. There are no measures on any of the jugs.

A further difficulty with means ends analysis as a heuristic for solving problems is that it is sometimes necessary to move further away from a goal in order to achieve a solution. For instance going to Milton Keynes station might actually take me further away from Trafalgar Square, and so be ruled out by a means ends strategy of reducing the distance between me and my goal. Yet going to Milton Keynes station may be a necessary part of my plan of action. One reason why the missionaries and cannibals problem is so difficult is that at one point it is necessary to take a missionary and cannibal back to the left bank from which they originally started, thus apparently *increasing* the distance from the final goal of getting them all over to the right bank.

Means ends analysis can be thought of as a top-down goal directed strategy for selecting actions which are evaluated in terms of narrowing the distance from the final goal. The major drawback is that a general problem-solving strategy of this kind grinds on relentlessly, regardless of any changing characteristics of a situation. When travelling from Milton Keynes to London, I need to be able to react to new circumstances. If there is a sudden snowstorm, my plans may suddenly have to be changed. New goals and subgoals may need to come into operation, like ringing the AA or borrowing some snowshoes. Yet it would obviously be daft to include all those possible actions in my normal travel plan, since the whole point is that they come into operation only in an emergency. Problem-solvers often have to resort to reacting to the current situation as best they can, hoping that the final goal will take care of itself.

Production systems

Means ends analysis can be contrasted with a more bottom-up approach in which people react to situations as they occur, rather than attempting to carry out a pre-planned sequence of actions based on a means ends analysis of the whole problem. Newell (1973) developed another type of computer program which simulates this reactive kind of problem-solving, known as production systems. The basic form of a 'production' is a rule which consists of a condition and an action: IF such and such a situation THEN do something. The IF clause represents the condition for an action. A simple example might be IF *I see clouds* THEN *take an umbrella*. One of the advantages claimed for productions is that they lead to appropriate actions in response to situations whether they are part of a plan or not. Suppose that, in the middle of tackling a waterjug problem in a psychological laboratory, a fire bell went off. Since running out of the laboratory would increase the distance between me and my goal of solving the problem, means ends analysis would encourage me to stay put. It would be more conducive to my survival if the fire bell automatically triggered a production rule IF *you hear a fire bell* THEN *run outside*.

Another advantage is that, unlike large-scale goal-directed plans, productions represent isolated pieces of knowledge which can be individually changed and adapted to deal with new situations. For instance in the light of further experience, a new production might be formulated, IF *I see clouds but the forecast predicts sunny weather* THEN *don't take an umbrella*. Similarly I could add new productions to my journey plans like IF *I see a taxi while I am waiting for a bus to Milton Keynes station and I am rather late* THEN *hail the taxi* or IF *it snows too hard* THEN *stay at home*. These new rules need not disturb my general overall strategy in relation to travel plans. This feature of productions is termed modularity. Each production is like a separate module; altering a single production should not interfere with other productions. In contrast, changing just one element of an integrated goal and subgoal structure might jeopardize the success of a means ends strategy. All the alternative operations of taking a bus or a taxi would have to be evaluated in terms of the time taken to reach the overall goal. The beauty of productions is that they allow for impulsive action.

Using productions to model problem-solving behaviour, a problem-solver's actions would be analysed as a set of rules for reacting to different states in the problem. In a waterjug problem there might be productions like IF *there is less water in one jug than the others* THEN *pour water into the jug with less water*. Typically computer programs contain sets of productions which make up entire production systems. The aim in developing a production system is to list all the productions which should be triggered at various stages in a problem. This means that productions will be triggered whenever a state occurs or reoccurs. This allows the production system to backtrack to earlier states, and to repeat actions in just the same messy way as human solvers do. In contrast, the aim of means ends analysis is a tidy process of dealing with one subgoal before proceeding to the next.

Production systems are particularly good for modelling problem-solving when various operations have to be used several times over in response to situations as they arise. A typical example is the research reported in Newell and Simon (1972) on cryptarithmetic problems. These are problems in which subjects have to allocate each of the letters to a *different* digit. A typical example, which was originally studied by Bartlett (1958), is the following problem in which the sum of DONALD and GERALD adds up to ROBERT, with the solver being given the initial information that the letter D = 5.

$$
\begin{array}{r}
\text{DONALD} \\
+ \underline{\text{GERALD}} \quad \text{Given D} = 5 \\
\text{ROBERT}
\end{array}
$$

Newell and Simon studied a single subject who said things like,

'Let's see . . . if D is 5, let me find a column with D in it . . . yes the right-hand column. Now $D + D = 5 + 5$ and so T must be 0 and 1 is carried to the next column. . . . Let's find another column with D in it. . . . In the left column if $D = 5$ and there is no carry to a new column the R must be 5, 6, 7, 8 or 9. . . . But suppose no . . . since D is 5, R must be 6, 7, 8 or 9.' The subject might then follow a blind alley until he says, 'No that won't do. There is a carry to the second column . . . so R can't be even . . . R must be a 7 or 9. . . . Let's see if there is another R . . . yes. . . .' Incidentally the subject was allowed to use paper and pencil to write down the solution as he went along.

With a problem like this, rather than being able to plan a once-for-all solution to reach the goal, the solver has a repertoire of actions suitable for dealing with each state of the problem. The point is that nothing can be planned in advance until the result of the previous calculation is known. This is the ideal setting for a production system in which each new state provides the condition for triggering the next action. Newell and Simon used their subject's verbal protocol to identify certain actions like locating a column, processing a column and assigning values to letters. These were represented in the form of productions indicating which conditions should lead to which actions. For instance IF *a digit is assigned to a letter* (*e.g.* $D = 5$) THEN *find a column with that letter in it*. This in turn becomes the condition for other actions like trying to add digits to achieve a possible sum, which in turn triggers productions for assigning a range of possible values to other letters. Simon (1979) claimed that the order of letter assignment which most solvers follow requires the least number of possibilities to be held in working memory simultaneously ($T = 0$, $E = 9$, $R = 7$, $A = 4$, $L = 8$, $G = 1$, $N = 6$, $B = 3$, $O = 2$).

One of the main attractions of production systems is that actions are taken in response to situations as they arise. This bottom-up responsiveness to changing situations is considered to be a strength of production systems. However, despite their plausibility, there is something of a tension between the wish to provide sets of productions which will lead to a correct problem solution, and the desire to simulate the less than perfect sequences of actions a particular solver might use. Bottom-up triggering of productions may be a good model for problems in which the selection of the next move depends on the outcome of the previous move. But even in the cryptarithmetic problem, it was taken for granted that a solver had in mind the main goal of discovering the correct digit for each letter. The essence of productions is that if a condition is matched, the action automatically follows. In the middle of writing these words because my current situation matched the condition IF *I feel like another sip of coffee and there is still coffee in the cup* this triggered the action THEN *pick the cup up and drink*. This production accurately modelled my behaviour; also my responses to other events in my environment, like turning on the electric fire if I feel cold. But nevertheless, despite all these distractions, I did manage to keep my mind on the main goal of finishing this chapter. I continued to fulfil the subgoals of using my pen to write word after word. Somehow people must be able to direct their actions towards a goal, rather than constantly reacting to everything which occurs in the environment. When does the sound of a bell become a legitimate call to action as opposed to a distraction to be ignored? Without some kind of control which allows actions to be evaluated, we would be completely at the mercy of the current environment.

Control of action: conflict resolution rules

The basic issue is the control of action. Leaving things to the chance operation of individual productions is a recipe for disorganized behaviour. Every time a situation matches the condition of a production, an action response would be activated. The advantage of being able to alter single productions has an exactly corresponding disadvantage. If behaviour is governed by millions of individual productions, all with different conditions, how is it possible to select a coherent strategy which leads to a planned sequence of actions? It is not surprising that researchers writing computer programs to model systematic problem-solving behaviour end up by developing integrated production systems which are geared to achieving a particular outcome, like solving the cryptarithmetic problem or ensuring that I finally end up in Trafalgar Square. Unfortunately the notion of a goal-directed production system begs the whole question of how the conditions for individual goal-directed actions are selected from all other aspects of the environment.

Within the production systems research area, this dilemma is considered under the heading of conflict resolution rules. These are necessary when a situation matches the condition of more than one production. Suppose there is a point in the cryptarithmetic problem when, after allocating tentative values to a letter, for example R = 6, 7, 8 or 9, there is more than one column with an R in it. This means that the condition IF *I have assigned a digit to a letter* will trigger more than one possible 'column inspecting' action. A real-life example is being asked to a party which may be the condition for several alternative actions, for example accept, refuse, say you will ring back later. Even more common is the situation when there are many events occurring simultaneously, each of which matches the conditions of a different production. In such a case, which aspect of the environment should be responded to? Suppose someone asks you to a party tonight but you also know that an essay has to be handed in tomorrow morning. The telephone call may match the condition of an 'accept' production; the knowledge about the essay may match the condition of a 'stay at home' production. Designers of production systems need to provide 'conflict resolution' rules to decide which of these productions should be triggered. In early production systems conflicts were decided by simple rules like selecting productions in a set order, avoiding repeating actions again, responding to the condition most recently entered into working memory. Productions which have led to good or bad consequences in the past are also more or less likely to be triggered. With the party example, according to the recency criterion, the recent telephone call would be more likely to win out as a condition for triggering the 'accept' action. But the 'adverse past consequences' criterion might point to the advisability of staying in to finish the essay.

These conflict resolution rules are meant to guide the selection of one action rather than another. But this merely shifts the problem up to the level of deciding which conflict resolution rule should apply. When should recency override the benefits of 'older' actions which have been successful in the past? Anderson (1983) took the problem of how to organize behaviour seriously. He suggested two overriding principles for selecting actions.

The first of these is when the condition of a production is more specific. An example would be IF *Peter asks me to a party* THEN *accept immediately*. The specific reference to Peter will take precedence over more general rules about how to respond to all invitations. But the even more specific condition, IF *Peter asks me to a party but I have an essay to write* THEN *stay at home* would favour this production over the others. The drawback of this criterion for conflict resolution is that one ends up with a mass of individual productions which have to be searched through until the most specific condition is located. As you can imagine, some of the specific conditions might get very complicated, for example IF *I am writing a book the dishwasher has flooded but my daughter is dealing with it and I have just drunk another cup of coffee* THEN *write the next word.*

What seems to be needed is some sort of glue to weld all these individual productions into co-ordinated sequences of actions. To achieve this aim, Anderson proposed a second much more radical way of resolving conflicts. This was to allow productions to set goals. This means that production systems can include rules for setting up goals and subgoals. One pretty obvious example given by Anderson is IF *the goal is to do a list of problems* THEN *set as a subgoal to do the first problem*. In the cryptarithmetic problem there might be a production like IF *you have allocated a digit to a letter* THEN *find the column with that letter in it which will give you most information towards solving the problem*. Productions which satisfy a current goal take precedence over all other productions, thus reflecting a focus of attention on a particular goal. The introduction of goals and subgoals into production systems brings an element of order into potential chaos. The setting of a goal to write an essay can be broken down into subgoals which involve productions for planning, writing and correcting. If the deadline for final corrections is tomorrow, then the actions necessary to satisfy this subgoal condition will be automatically triggered. In other words, the analysis of goals and subgoals typical of means ends analysis has been imposed on production systems. The general means ends analysis heuristic could be realized as the production IF *an action reduces the distance towards achieving a current goal or subgoal* THEN *perform that action*. More specific goal-directed productions might take the form of IF *taking a missionary and a cannibal across the river would result in more cannibals than missionaries on either bank* THEN *reject this move.*

The crucial point at issue is how people select among alternative actions when working on problems. The imposition of top-down goal-directed organized plans on production systems, necessary as it may be to explain co-ordinated sequences of action, nevertheless sits very uneasily with the concept of matching current situations with the conditions of individual productions. Moreover, the productions which set up goals are themselves responses triggered by situations in which a goal should be established. What is needed is a 'meta' conflict resolution rule to decide which goals should be set up and how they should be broken down into subgoals. It also leaves quite unresolved the original insight which productions were designed to model, namely that goal-directed productions should sometimes be ignored in order to respond to more urgent situations. If a fire bell triggers a condition which is not related to the current goal, it would now be rejected in favour of a production which appears more relevant to the current goal of solving a waterjug problem.

Evaluation of general purpose problem-solving models

The first point to be made is that the information processing framework is meant to encompass all human behaviour. The ability to co-ordinate actions to achieve a goal is reflected in heuristic strategies like means ends analysis and the operation of conflict resolution rules. The belief in general methods for solving problems is revealed in the very name of Newell and Simon's GPS (General Problem Solver). Anderson (1983) attempted to explain all problem-solving in terms of what he called a production systems cognitive architecture, which was intended to explain 'the basic principles of operation built into the cognitive system'. The universality of productions as a device for representing information processing strategies is demonstrated by the fact that Simon (1975) used productions to model three quite different strategies for solving the Tower of Hanoi problem: first, a top-down means ends strategy for solving goals and subgoals; second, a bottom-up strategy of responding to the perceptual configurations of rings on pegs; third, a rote-learned pattern of set moves.

One problem with so much flexibility is that it is all too easy to make up productions to suit any piece of behaviour. In fact you must have noticed from some of my examples that a definite weakness of productions is the facility with which they can be created, often in order to state the exceedingly obvious. An example from Anderson (1983) includes a production for answering the question: 'Is A before D in the string A B C D E F?' The proposed production for solving order problems is as follows:

IF asked 'Is X before Y?' and X is before Y
THEN respond 'yes'

Surely this simply begs the question of how people make decisions that one or other item comes first.

The claims for general problem-solving operations are fine at an abstract level. At this level it is plausible to characterize problem-solving as involving a mixture of strategies, some actions being determined by goal directedness and others by attention to changing circumstances. If the path to a solution is clear, people are likely to use a means ends analysis to reduce their distance from that goal; in other circumstances responding to a changing situation may be more appropriate. At this moment I may simultaneously be tackling the goal of writing this book and also responding to a temporary thirst for tea. Simon (1979) gives the nice example that production rules triggered in response to patterns of chess pieces would not model really good chess, but might be an accurate representation of games when very rapid moves are required, a situation in which even chess grandmasters play in a less planned way.

Knowledge and problem-solving schemas

What has been left out of account so far is the different experiences which people bring to different tasks. Means ends analysis is supposed to be typical of all problem-solving by all problem-solvers. In fact Simon presents it as a general characteristic of human thinking which can, in principle, be applied to any problem. Selection of actions which lead towards desired goals are considered to be a universal feature of human behaviour, even though we may not always approve of other people's ends or of the means they use to achieve them.

The strong implication is that it is only limitations in working memory capacity that prevents humans from applying means ends strategies in all cases. Leaving aside the tricky question of whether some people have larger working memories than others, there is another factor which has to be taken into account. The ability to implement a problem-solving strategy depends on knowledge. Thinking mechanisms may be universal but solvers are categorized as experts or novices when dealing with different problem situations. As its simplest level, in order to identify goals and subgoals a solver needs to know the rules of the Tower of Hanoi or the different modes of transport from Milton Keynes to London. A fire bell will trigger a response only if the rules of fire drill are already known. From this point of view one would expect to find differences between problem-solvers depending on their expertise. The notion of expertise is, of course, more far-reaching than a simple knowledge of the rules of a problem. As Chase and Simon (1973) demonstrated with chess experts, expert players view game positions in large chunks which represent possible patterns of moves. The fact that master chess players were no better at recalling random arrays of pieces suggests that there is nothing special about their working memory capacities. The gain from expertise is that it places *less* strain on working memory because problem-solving strategies are already available. We come back to the slogan 'the more you know, the less you have to think'.

Another way of expressing the distinction between experts and novices is to say that experts have efficient problem-solving schemas for dealing with situations that fall within the domain of their expertise. Sometimes experts know exactly how to deal with a situation, in which case we would hardly say that a problem exists. If you look back to the 'levels of problem-solving' in Chapter 2, you will see that experts could be expected to know certain facts (level 1) and also precise rules (algorithms) for producing solutions (level 2). They are also likely to have picked up skills (level 3) and general problem-solving methods (level 4), even though some thought might have to go into selecting particular examples at level 4. It is only at level 5 that the expert would have to put on his thinking cap. But even then, prior experience of designing car parts, or of puzzles like the Duncker radiation problem, might be formulated as problem-solving schemas to guide the search for new solutions.

The difficulty is to explain how people recognize which problem-solving schemas are relevant to the current situation. We are constantly having to make decisions to cope with big and little problems: whether to move to a new house; whether to go to a party; whether to move a ring to a peg in the Tower of Hanoi puzzle; how to get to Trafalgar Square from Milton Keynes; whether to buy a real tree or an artificial Christmas tree. Undoubtedly previous problem-solving experiences influence all these decisions. But the question is which problem-solving schemas are most relevant? When making a decision about a Christmas tree, seeing an analogy with other occasions, when a dust-pan and brush have been needed, might tip the decision towards an artificial tree. But an analogy with previous pleasant traditional occasions may favour the real tree, despite the needles dropping all over the carpet. So a lot depends on which stored problem-solving schemas are activated. Under what circumstances do people see analogies between current and past situations?

Gick and Holyoak (1980) conducted a series of studies using Duncker's radiation problem in which they investigated the factors which might encourage people to spot analogies between similar situations. One story they used was about a general who needed all his men to attack a central fortress although he could send only small groups along each of several mined roads to the fortress in the centre. If you reread the description of the Duncker radiation problem in Chapter 2, you will notice that, despite superficial differences, both stories rely on a 'dispersion' notion of sending a few men/rays along many routes so that they converge in the centre. Gick and Holyoak found that the subjects taking part in their experiments were helped to solve the radiation problem if, and only if, they spotted the analogy between the two stories. Few subjects saw the analogy spontaneously; most needed hints and exposure to several similar stories. For instance reading more than one analogy story, or a hint that the first story might be useful for solving the Duncker problem, encouraged more people to perceive the analogy. Experiments on the transfer of problem-solving strategies from problems like the Missionaries and Cannibals and the Tower of Hanoi to problems with identical or similar rule structures have also shown that transfer effects depend on subjects appreciating, or being told about, the essential similarities between the problems (Reed, Ernst and Banerji, 1974).

How are problems represented?

The issue of appreciating the relevance of problem-solving schemas so that they can act as aids for future problem-solving is one of the central topics in cognitive psychology. From Gick and Holyoak's work it is clear that a lot depends on how people represent problems. If subjects formed mental representations of the fortress and Duncker problems at a sufficiently 'deep' level they could see the similarities between them. It is only at this level that they were able to abstract a general problem-solving schema for dealing with all 'dispersion' problems. Once they have developed such a schema they can apply it to all new problems of this type. They will have become experts in solving these problems. What Gick and Holyoak don't discuss is the extremely limited value of this expertise in view of the vanishingly small probability of being faced with such problems in real life, as opposed to a psychological laboratory!

It is clear, then, that the question of how problems are represented is crucial from the point of view of recognizing similarities between old and new problems. Gick and Holyoak (1980) talk in terms of mapping a representation of a current problem structure with that of a previous experience. It is essential that this mapping is carried out at a level which reveals relevant similarities. If too much attention is paid to the superficial characteristics of the radiation and fortress stores, the identical principles underlying their solutions may escape notice. If two problems which are objectively similar are represented as two quite separate mental problem spaces, it will be impossible to spot any helpful analogies between them.

In order to investigate people's mental representations of problem spaces, Hayes and Simon (1974) gave subjects different written instructions for tackling the Tower of Hanoi rings and pegs problem. Unlike previous researchers, Hayes and Simon recorded verbal protocols of what their subjects said from the time they started to read the instructions, instead of waiting until subjects had learned the rules and even done some practice problems, as had been done in earlier experiments. Hayes and Simon found that some versions of the instructions helped subjects to form representations which aided the solution process; other versions of exactly the same problem made the solution very difficult to discover. Over fifty years before, Ewert and Lambert (1932) had studied the effects of different instructions on subjects' representations of the Tower of Hanoi. One group of subjects were asked to learn a set of verbal instructions, for example move one ring to the left, another to the right, similar to Simon's (1975) rote-learned move pattern strategy. This group solved the problem very quickly at the time but it is a moot point whether their mental representations could be said to reflect a real understanding of the structure of the problem. It certainly seems unlikely that they would have developed a systematic problem-solving schema which would have helped them to tackle similar problems. The idea behind this line of research is that people's problem-solving performance will be determined by their mental representations of a problem space.

Clearly the way a problem is described has a very important effect on the way people formulate possible solutions. But, as Gick and Holyoak and others have shown, equally important is their experiences with similar problems. Experts may see a goal clearly while novices react to surface features of a task. Chi, Feltovich and Glaser (1981) found that experts categorize physics problems in terms of deep underlying principles, whereas novices group them according to the particular objects mentioned in the surface formulation of problems. The 'deep' representations of the physics experts reflected problem-solving schemas organized around strategies for attaining solutions. Consequently for the experts selecting an appropriate solution method was a trivial problem. Their expert knowledge enabled them to represent new problems in a form that made the solution transparently obvious. In contrast, novices ran into difficulties because they had grouped together problems which, despite superficial similarities, required different kinds of solutions.

Similar results have been found for experts and novices in other domains, for example more experienced and less experienced computer programmers (Adelson, 1981). The conclusion is that experts are able to apply their knowledge at the stage of representing problems in such a way as to bring out similarities between past and present solutions.

I would suggest, although it may seem somewhat paradoxical, that relying on learned knowledge of problems with similar solutions can be a hallmark of creativity. It is creative people who are most likely to say 'That reminds me of a book I read', 'That's just like the time I did this or that', 'What about trying out such and such a solution?' Two experts in designing cars may have an equally wide-ranging knowledge of engineering and metals. The more 'creative' may see analogies between cars and fish, leading to the addition of fins or the design of an amphibious car. Of course, creativity requires adapting old solutions to fit new circumstances. The blinkered expert who sticks to problems with well-known solutions may lag behind a novice who is fast at seeing potential new solutions. The tension between exploiting old, well-tried problem-solving schemas, so typical of expert performance, as opposed to the benefits of being suddenly reminded of a bizarre analogy, which may or may not shift thinking into a new gear, remains an inevitable dilemma in human problem-solving.

Conclusions

To sum up, basic information processing operations, like means ends analysis and the triggering of productions, have to be fleshed out with knowledge of specific problem-solving schemas based on previous experiences. The activation of problem-solving schemas depends on recognizing relevant analogies between current problems and past situations, a process which may be more or less creative. The little puzzles favoured by problem-solving researchers tend to play down the role of prior experiences. So it should not be too surprising that, in the absence of specific problem-solving schemas, subjects tend to fall back on general problem-solving methods.

Another big difference between experimental puzzles and real-life problems is that the problems we encounter in real life are usually very ill defined. It is not always clear what the goal is, much less which operations which would lead to success. In day-to-day existence there are many goals in play, some short term, like finishing this sentence, others very long term, like worrying about future career prospects. Neisser (1986) drew attention to the overlapping nature of human goals and the importance of attention and memory in keeping track of them all. Like Norman (1981), he believes that plans are nested within each other, so that the constituent actions required to achieve high-level goals are often run off automatically. The strokes of a pen or a typewriter to produce letters are subordinated to the planning needed to express a meaning. This is basically a top-down model of problem-solving. On the other hand, unexpected events, like a typewriter key sticking, can lead to other goals being temporarily neglected, a process which is more naturally modelled by the bottom-up responsiveness of production rules. It is no wonder that it has proved so difficult to identify a single kind of thinking as being conducive to the solving of all types of problems.

On top of this are individual differences in knowledge and motivation. Despite their reliance on the verbal protocols of individual subjects, researchers use these to draw general conclusions about the kinds of strategies adopted by all problem-solvers. However, individuals react very differently in problem-solving experiments, some continuing to wrestle with problems, others accepting hints, others giving up altogether. The motivation to complete problems, which is taken for granted when psychology students are acting as subjects in their lecturers' experiments, may be one of the most important determiners of performance in real life. Perhaps because problem-solving is such a constant feature of human behaviour, it has not proved easy to specify the principles underlying mental representations of problems and the selection of problem-solving strategies, even in laboratory tasks. Some outstanding issues include the following:

1 What is the relation between general problem-solving operations, which apply to all problems, and specific problem-solving schemas for dealing with particular types of problems?
2 Under what circumstances do people notice analogies between past and current problems so that they can apply known solutions to new problems?

3 How do experts and novices differ in the way they represent problems and apply solutions?
4 How can the flexibility of productions in response to immediate situations be reconciled with the need for goal-directed problem-solving strategies?
5 What underlies the creative ability to apply 'old' problem-solving schemas to 'new' problems?

9

Learning, acting and speaking

The emphasis in the previous chapter was on the importance of knowledge in selecting appropriate problem-solving strategies. Knowledge guides interpretations of new problem experiences and, at the same time, knowledge is built up from accumulated past experiences. In psychology more attention has been paid to the role of general knowledge in generating the inferences necessary to make sense of new inputs from the environment, less to the role of individual experiences in increasing general knowledge. In the discussion of semantic and episodic memory in Chapter 3 it was suggested that individual episodes gradually become absorbed into general semantic knowledge. The first few experiences of travelling by train, for example, may seem unique but in the end a succession of train journeys contributes to general knowledge about how to buy tickets and look up timetables. A child can be said to 'know' addition only if he or she can generalize from many experiences of individual additions to a state of being able to add up any set of numbers. Conventionally the acquisition of knowledge and skills is treated under the heading of learning. Sometimes learning seems automatic, as in the case of learning to talk or gradually acquiring information about train journeys. Sometimes it involves a lot of effort on the part of pupils and teachers. In this chapter I shall be concentrating on skills which seem to emerge gradually and automatically, whereas in Chapter 10 the focus will be on teaching facts and training skills.

What is learning?

The odd thing is that, since the bad old days of behaviourism, psychologists have paid relatively little attention to theories of learning. In reaction to the notion that learning consists of direct links between stimulus inputs and behavioural responses, cognitive psychologists have stressed the importance of complex mental representations of knowledge. Researchers into problem-solving have studied the mental representations of experts and novices (for example Chi, Feltovich and Glaser, 1981) and the effects of past experiences on the development of problem-solving schemas (Gick and Holyoak, 1980). But it is no easy matter to specify the mechanisms by which new experiences are integrated into old knowledge.

For computer programs to work, information and instructions have to be entered into the database by the programmer. In contrast, human infants start off as archetypal novices. They have the great advantage of being equipped with a human brain, which makes them initially responsive to many aspects of the environment. But as far as experience of the world is concerned, they are beginners. Nevertheless in a relatively short period, most babies eventually become experts in coping with the environment. Perhaps this is why people tend to equate learning with childhood. It is during this period that most conventional learning occurs; a child learns to talk, to read and write, to do arithmetic, to learn about history and science. Significantly people who leave school early are often categorized as 'dropping out' of the educational process, although there is increasing acknowledgement of the need for continuous education throughout life, and for training and retraining in new technologies. Whether one is talking about learning to ride a bicycle, learning to play chess, learning to use a word processor or learning about local history, the emphasis is on learning defined sets of facts and skills. But it is much more difficult to study day-to-day learning from experience. The ability to express opinions clearly, familiarity with a local community of shops and services, acquiring a nose for a bargain, diagnosing the cause of a defective piece of machinery, recognizing a hostile situation, all these are skills which are learnt incrementally, almost imperceptibly, from personal experiences. It is not surprising that it is notoriously difficult to pass on this kind of learning by direct teaching. Education is far better at teaching facts than procedures for action.

Declarative knowledge and procedural knowledge

The distinction between knowledge of facts and knowledge of procedures for action has been emphasized by Anderson (1983). Anderson's theory of learning depends on the notion that long-term permanent memory is divided into declarative memory and procedural memory. Declarative memory contains all the facts we know and procedural memory contains procedures for the actions we know how to perform. Figure 20 shows the different parts of memory within Anderson's general theory of cognition, which he calls ACT (Adaptive Control Theory).

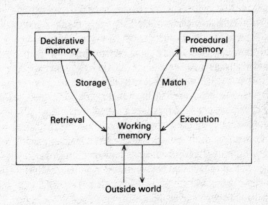

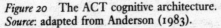

Figure 20 The ACT cognitive architecture.
Source: adapted from Anderson (1983).

Declarative memory is equivalent to the knowledge structures described by other psychologists. It is important to note that it includes both semantic knowledge (for example general expectations about what happens in restaurants) and recently encoded episodes (*Bill hit Jim in a McDonalds restaurant*). These 'tangled hierarchies of cognitive units', as Anderson called them, represent information in the form of networks containing semantic and episodic information. It is as if a Collins and Quillian network included both semantic information, *canaries are birds*, and episodic information, *my canary died last week*. A mixed semantic network showing both kinds of information – general semantic facts (for example animals breathe air) and episodic facts (for example Arthur works at the University of California) – is shown in Figure 21.

Another similarity with network models is that the method for retrieving items in declarative memory is by spreading activation. When a new input occurs, this activates associative links in the same way that the sentence *A canary is a bird* activates the 'canary' and 'bird' concepts in a Collins and Quillian network. So as far as declarative memory is concerned, Anderson's theory is similar to other models of memory in that it includes schema-like representations of all the factual knowledge we have acquired about the world. Furthermore, as with other psychological models, declarative facts are thought of as statements which can be expressed in words. Despite acknowledging the possibility of purely visual images, facts are normally represented in the form of verbal statements, *a canary is a bird, coffee is for drinking*. The implication is that, because declarative facts are statable in a verbal form, we can become consciously aware of them. Although facts are stored as passive memories, the assumption is that they can be dredged up when necessary in response to questions and statements like *A canary is a yellow bird*. While the processes responsible for being reminded of facts are not themselves amenable to conscious introspection, the products of these memories can be thought of as 'knowable' facts. This distinction between conscious factual information and automatic actions is important for the discussion of procedural memory.

The novelty in Anderson's theory was the inclusion of procedural memory as a distinct component of memory.

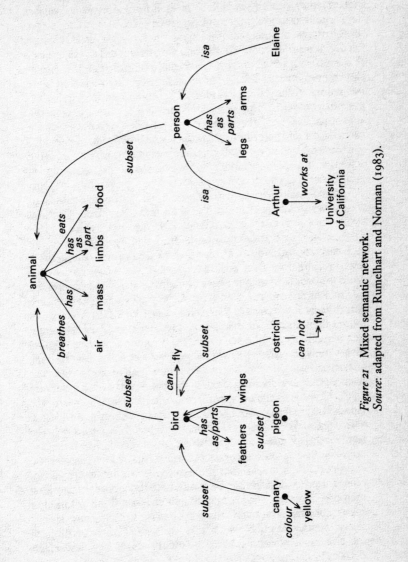

Figure 21 Mixed semantic network.
Source: adapted from Rumelhart and Norman (1983).

Anderson argued that a 'rain' schema stored in declarative memory may indeed provide a lot of information which might help a person to interpret a 'rainy' situation. But it would not in itself trigger the action of picking up an umbrella. What is needed is a production like the one already quoted in Chapter 8, IF *I see clouds* THEN *take an umbrella*. The procedural memory shown in Figure 20 is full of productions representing conditions for actions. When the condition of a production is matched in the environment, rainy clouds or the sound of a fire bell, the appropriate action is triggered, picking up an umbrella or running out of the building. In other words procedural memory is responsible for all actions. The issue of how to organize actions into coherent sequences of behaviour aimed at achieving goals is relevant here. Most of Anderson's production systems consist of goal-directed production systems, the difficulties of which were discussed under the heading of 'Control of action: conflict resolution rules' in Chapter 8. We shall return to this problematic issue after considering the relationship between the fact-based information in declarative memory and the action-based productions in procedural memory.

So far productions have been thought of as being triggered by external inputs from the outside world, for example clouds, fire bells, the configuration of pieces on a chess board. In Anderson's model the contents of declarative memory can also be brought into play. Thus an external input, for example a pattern of chess pieces, may activate (retrieve) memories of similar configurations in declarative memory. If external inputs and/or items retrieved from declarative memory match the condition of a production rule, the action will be executed. Suppose I look out and see clouds, this external input will match the condition IF *I see clouds* and trigger the action THEN *take an umbrella*. However, the sight of the clouds may also activate a fact lodged in declarative memory that today's forecast predicted sunny weather despite early rain. This means that the external input of seeing clouds plus a stored declarative fact will both be active in working memory. Together these may match the condition of another (more specific) production IF *I see clouds but the forecast predicts sunny weather* THEN *don't take an umbrella*. According to the theory, new inputs have the dual role of activating facts in declarative memory, and of matching the conditions of productions in procedural memory.

Another important characteristic of the productions in procedural memory is that they are automatically triggered whenever their conditions are met. The search for a declarative fact may result from a conscious memory search – what did I hear about rain in yesterday's weather forecast? But the production itself is supposed to occur spontaneously. After many experiences of rain, picking up an umbrella rather than a watering can is an automatic procedure. So the fact that in psychology textbooks productions have to be expressed in IF/THEN verbal statements should not detract from the notion of problem-solving as consisting of well-learned automatic procedures, such as using a pen to write letters or picking up an umbrella.

Learning new procedures

The next question which needs to be considered is how new procedures come to be learned. An infant starts with no knowledge about what to do when it sees clouds or hears a fire bell. A novice chess player would not recognize that the pattern of pieces on a chess board matches the conditions of production rules like IF *your king is in check* THEN *make a move which either moves the king away or interposes another piece.* Even less would the novice be able to put together an organized strategy for selecting individual 'moving pieces' productions. Despite all the conscious mental effort which goes into playing chess, patterns of pieces automatically appear to the chess master as a trigger for whole sequences of possible actions. So where do productions come from and how do they get organized into goal-directed production systems? Anderson's theory of declarative and procedural knowledge was designed to explain how novices gradually learn expert procedures.

The starting-point is that declarative knowledge about facts does not in itself provide a basis for action. Reading the instructions for constructing a do-it-yourself cupboard or studying a computer manual is not at all the same thing as being able to build the cupboard or to write a computer program. It is a crucial feature of Anderson's theory that there are no direct links between declarative memory and production memory. In Figure 20 working memory is the only place where information from declarative memory and from procedural memory can interact. Working memory is also the only window on to the outside world through which new inputs can be stored in declarative memory. This stems from Anderson's belief that productions cannot be learnt directly from experience. Instead new inputs have to be filtered through declarative memory before they can be retrieved into working memory in order to be translated into procedures for action. Anderson suggests that little harm is done by adding to declarative knowledge, since this is 'all in the mind'. It doesn't matter whether a child believes in magic; however, the too-ready translation of this into new procedures for action could lead to disaster. A child who expects to wave a magic wand or an adult who takes everything they hear as an instruction for action might well get into trouble.

Another more revealing reason for caution in adding new productions is the delicate nature of combining productions into production systems. Anderson's aim was to write production systems which mirror goal-directed problem-solving, complete with conflict resolution rules for deciding on appropriate actions. Adding a new superficially attractive production for dealing with a particular aspect of a problem may be a distraction from the main goal of solving the problem. Allowing a production to be acquired in response to, say, a particular incident that arises in a driving lesson may be detrimental to the acquisition of the general driving skills necessary for passing a driving test. One paradox about all this is that, as I pointed out in the discussion of production systems in Chapter 8, the initial enthusiasm for productions arose from the ease with which they could be altered in order to adapt behaviour to new circumstances. Anderson takes exactly the opposite line that it is declarative knowledge that can easily be changed. Changes in behaviour are slow and should be protected from sudden shifts.

For this reason Anderson (1983) proposed a four-stage model for learning procedures. A prior condition for learning is the storage of inputs as representations in declarative memory. In the second stage, very general problem-solving productions interpret declarative facts, statements and instructions in order to generate more specific productions. This stage of production formation of actions is a slow one because declarative information has to be retrieved into working memory every time a production is triggered. The third stage of proceduralization can occur only during this action stage, reflecting the adage that one can learn a skill only by doing it. As skills become less dependent on referring back to declarative facts and instructions, productions specific to the particular task are entered into procedural memory. Performance speeds up as automatic productions take over from general interpretative problem-solving strategies. As part of a knowledge compilation process, productions start being collapsed together to provide short-cut automatic methods for carrying out a task. In the fourth and final stage, production systems are 'finely tuned' to restrict them to the class of problems for which they are suitable.

Anderson wrote a set of productions to model how students learned from a geometry textbook which described the correct method for giving reasons for each step in a proof. On the basis of their verbal protocols while tackling problems, Anderson concluded that, at first, his four students tried to interpret the declarative information given in the textbook by using general problem-solving interpretative productions for trying out each method. Students would take a particular reason from an example given in the textbook and test to see if it were appropriate for a new problem. Later, the students developed specific methods, as if they had internalized appropriate problem-solving procedures without needing to refer constantly back to the textbook. The process of learning a skill is defined as replacing cumbersome general strategies with efficient task-specific productions, resulting from the combination of hitherto separate actions into coherent problem-solving procedures. Finally, the students should become expert enough to realize when the methods they had been taught were appropriate and when other methods should be used. At this stage they would be like the physics experts studied by Chi, Feltovich and Glaser (1981) who grouped together problems with similar solutions. It is interesting, though, that one of Anderson's four students was much faster at going through the four learning stages than the other three students.

One difficulty with this otherwise very plausible theory is how learners know which productions should be combined together to develop a coherent procedure. For instance Anderson suggests that a child would somehow know that it was inappropriate to combine the three following productions as part of a single procedure:

IF the subgoal is to add a digit in a column THEN set as a subgoal to add the digit to the running total

IF I hear footsteps in the aisle THEN teacher is coming my way

IF the goal is to add two digits and the result is the sum of the two digits THEN the result is the sum.

Instead, all the goals and subgoals to do with arithmetic should be grouped together into a single consistent production system. The motivation for compiling organized goal structures in order to guide the selection of appropriate productions is obvious enough. Nevertheless people do seem to be capable of pursuing more than one goal at a time (Neisser, 1986). Perhaps, too, Anderson does not make enough allowance for people's tendency to be distracted by the footsteps of a teacher, or for the development of what Skinner calls superstitious behaviour resulting from the chance reinforcement of irrelevant actions. People are notoriously bad at critical path analysis, often only searching for solutions when needed. Sometimes, too, attention to interruptions, an open mind to new inputs is necessary for survival, and incidentally may lead to creative insights. In any case it is not at all clear what a teacher could do to help. To caricature Anderson's ACT rather unkindly, the child's behaviour might trigger the production IF *children are distracted by my footsteps* THEN *tell them not to include this in their production system for adding up digits*.

Another unanswered question is where the general interpretative productions necessary to apply declarative knowledge come from in the first place. Presumably the presentation of a new problem meets the conditions of general problem-solving productions like IF *I read instructions about the rules of a game* THEN *only try moves which conform to these rules* or IF *an action reduces the distance towards achieving a current goal or subgoal* THEN *perform that action* or IF *a problem seems analogous to an earlier problem* THEN *adapt a previous solution to the current task*.

These are, of course, exactly equivalent to the general problem-solving strategies and heuristics like means ends analysis and analogies which were discussed in Chapter 8. To formulate these strategies as general interpretative productions simply begs the question of how appropriate problem-solving schemas are selected to deal with a variety of problems.

Procedures and principles

Another characteristic of ACT as a model of learning is that it perpetuates the notion of separate stores in the memory system. According to Figure 20 declarative facts do not have any direct link with the productions in procedural memory, nor can procedures be transformed back into a declarative format. However, it seems more helpful to think of declarative memory and procedural memory as representing a continuum of different kinds of knowledge. At one extreme, there may be completely procedural skills. For instance it is impossible to give declarative instructions about how to ride a bicycle. This is an example of a skill which is taught directly by being trundled round on a bicycle. At the other extreme, some facts may be permanently stored as declarative facts, for example my knowledge of Greek myths. Other skills emerge as a fusion of declarative and procedural knowledge, for example learning to write good essays. Moreover, as Mandler (1985) pointed out, we are not totally incapable of talking about actions. While the actual mechanisms may not be accessible to conscious thought, skills themselves can be represented in a declarative form. For instance it is possible to make statements about actions like 'driving home', 'tying shoe-laces', 'solving a geometry problem', even if one cannot describe all the component actions that make up these skills. Mandler talks about these verbalized representations of actions as secondary representations, in order to indicate that they are derived from primary actions.

These secondary representations can act as verbalized principles for monitoring the appropriateness of actions. Declarative representations of procedures can guide the development of better strategies for action. They can also become the basis for acquiring new problem-solving schemas which depend on identifying similarities between situations. Once a production system has been developed for doing one geometry problem, it is helpful to be able to think and talk about its suitability for dealing with other problems. A novice apprentice asks questions as well as watching an expert. Without the possibility of talking about actions and formulating general principles to aid learning, action sequences would become completely inflexible. After all, it is the use of language to formulate plans for action and to discuss outcomes that differentiates human learning from that of other species. It may be true that the proceduralization of automatic action sequences protects experts from the need to think but they will hardly retain their expertise if pre-programmed action sequences are impervious to new thinking and knowledge.

Anderson admits that it is difficult to see how automatic procedural skills, once learnt, can be monitored and changed (Neves and Anderson, 1981). In Anderson's theory of procedural learning all the traffic is one-way with declarative knowledge being transformed into specific productions which are triggered automatically when their conditions are matched. While feedback from the environment may directly influence the selection of productions, there is no room for the indirect influence of declarative information on the resetting of goals and the adoption of new procedures. The original motivation for procedural learning was to learn how to cope with new experiences. But the question is, at what stage are new experiences considered sufficiently 'new' to give rise to new declarative facts which in turn will trigger new procedures? Anderson's theory of learning leaves us with the familiar dilemma of how to reconcile creative adaptiveness to novel situations with the need to run off automatic goal-directed procedures which are protected from intrusions from irrelevant inputs. Human experts rely on a large repertoire of relevant procedures and yet they are capable of tailoring their actions to changes in the environment.

Learning language productions: a case study

One of Anderson's aims was to write a set of productions which could turn 'thoughts' into speech. It is interesting that, because of the 'active' nature of productions, Anderson's model of language is geared towards the production of utterances. Some typical linguistic productions include:

(a) If the goal is to communicate a meaning structure of the form: action agent object

THEN set as subgoals

1 To describe agent
2 To describe action
3 To describe object

(b) IF the goal is to describe an object and the listener already knows which object is being referred to

THEN set as subgoals

1 To generate *the*
2 To describe object

These productions are part of a much larger production system designed to produce sentences which express meaning structures like 'eat John hamburger'. The first production (a) ensures that subgoals are set up to reflect the normal word order for English of agent-action-object (*John eat hamburger*). The second production (b) requires the use of *the* when the listener knows a given topic, to reflect the distinction between *John ate the hamburger* and *John ate a hamburger*. Other production rules introduce grammatical features and provide slots into which words can be inserted according to the current 'thoughts' in working memory. The sight of John eating a hamburger or a memory of such an event would trigger the production of sentences like *John is eating a hamburger* or *I remember how much John likes guzzling hamburgers*. Finally, transformations into passives and questions would have their own productions to move words around.

I hope it is obvious that this enterprise is just the same as Chomsky's attempt to write the linguistic rules which will generate all possible grammatical sentences into English and no incorrect word sequences (see Chapter 5). If you consider any but the simplest of sentences, productions run into all the same horrendous problems as any other attempts to represent the rules of a natural language like English. For instance there would need to be a whole set of 'question transformation' productions to cope with different types of questions, including *Will John eat the hamburger? What did John eat? Are hamburgers what John likes?* The problem is how to write in all the conditions which would permit one transformation to be used rather than another to prevent ungrammatical utterances like *Eating John a hamburger?*

Anderson (1983) reports an interesting computer simulation of language learning in which the computer program started off with no knowledge of syntax but was fed meaning structures. The program's task was to deduce linguistic rules so that it could generate an appropriate sentence to represent each meaning structure. After each incorrect utterance, the computer program was given feedback in the form of the correct 'target' sentence. In order that the program could compare each meaning structure and target sentence, the target sentences were pre-chunked into syntactic categories which directly reflected 'deep-structure' meanings. The meaning structures included all the semantic relations necessary to generate a target sentence, indicating the number of the subject, the tense and modal attributes of the verb. With all this help, after several hundred examples of meaning structure/generated sentence/target sentence triples, the program managed to deduce linguistic rules which enabled it to produce approximations to real sentences, like *The doctor may tickled the funny farmer* and *Who may be shooted by some good lawyers?* (see Figure 22). Although it found it difficult to appreciate all the niceties of the English language, the program was interesting in that it learned (that is improved its performance) on the basis of the feedback it received.

Anderson admits that the performance of this language acquisition program was not very childlike. In one sense it was too complex. It started by trying to pair complex meanings and complete sentence formulations, in order to arrive at a full set of syntactic rules. On the other hand, a child, although limited to very short utterances, has the enormous advantage of knowing what the words refer to in the outside world. For the computer simulation, *farmers*, *doctors* and *boys* were simply arbitrary labels. The fact that good lawyers don't usually shoot people was not part of its knowledge, whereas one of the first things a child learns is how to distinguish between the good guys and the bad guys.

Sentence number	Sentence generated by ACT	Feedback from target sentence
1	tall boy	the boy s are tall
2	shoot the boy s lawyer	the boy shoot s a lawyer
3	dance the lady	the lady dance ed
6	jump the farmer	the farmer s jump ed
7	good the lawyer	the lawyer s are good
9	the lawyer s jump ed	the lawyer s jump ed
10	the lawyer s dance ed	the lawyer dance s
14	kiss the farmer a boy	the farmer s are kiss ing the boy s
117	the tall lawyer has is jump ing	the tall lawyer has been jump ing
170	some farmer s hit ed the lady	some farmer s hit the lady
208	the doctor may tickle ed the funny farmer	the doctor may tickle the funny farmer
358	the sailor s may are being bad	the sailor s may be being bad
472	who was the funny lawyer being hit ed by	who was the funny lawyer being hit by
632	the funny sailor s is kissed by the bad boy	the funny sailor s are kiss ed by the bad boy
751	who have run ed	who have run
770	the girl has run ed	the girl has run
790	are some doctor s being hit ed by some lady s	are some doctor s being hit by some lady s
806	has a sailor run ed	has a sailor run
811	who may be shoot ed by some good lawyer s	who may be shot by some good lawyer s
815	the angry boy can being bad	the angry boy can be bad
824	the smart lady s may run ed	the smart lady s may run
835	some men dance	some men dance ed
838	some tall girl s may shoot ed the angry sailor	some tall girl s may shoot the angry sailor
843	would the boy s have run ed	would the boy s have run

Figure 22 Sample sentences generated by ACT.
Source: adapted from Anderson (1983).

Anderson designed another production system to simulate the early language development of his son (J.J.). Pairings of one-word, and later two-word and three-word, utterances and meanings were inserted into the database as and when J.J. uttered them. Limitations were built in so that initially the program could produce only two syllables at a time and it was sometimes given incorrect feedback. The computer program was reasonably successful at reflecting J.J.'s performance at the stage when he had a relatively small number of utterance types at his command, for example to express requests, *up J.J.* or *more*. But by the time several thousands of J.J.'s utterances had been fed in, the SUMEX INTERLISP computer system had no memory space left. Of course, J.J. had no such limitations. After a few months, and many many thousand utterances later, he was able to use the inflections, question transformations and other complexities of the syntactic apparatus of English to convey meanings, and to use pragmatic inferences about speakers' intentions in a way that no computer program has yet been able to match. The J.J. simulation reflects the initial slow learning process by which a child maps very simple language structures on to objects and events in the environment. Anderson quotes a nice example of the parental triumph he and his wife felt when J.J. realized that words he already knew for describing objects, for example *nana* for banana, could also be used to express requests instead of pointing, for example *more nana*.

The first of Anderson's simulations, which attempted to map whole sentences on to meaning structures, is much more like a linguist's conception of language acquisition. The pairings between 'deep' meaning structures and 'surface' target sentences were attempted without any general knowledge about likely events to guide the generation of sentences. This is just the situation in which Chomsky argued the need for universal linguistic constraints to prevent a language learning system from generating too many incorrect strings of words. Anderson suggests that such constraints could be written into the system as complex conditions for production rules. But either of these proposed solutions results in an arbitrarily complex set of rules for selecting grammatical sentences. It seems worthwhile pursuing the alternative view, that it is children's knowledge of the world that guides their selection of appropriate utterances.

Only gradually, as a result of interactions with other people, and later from reading books, does a language learner come to mirror the full grammatical structure of a language. The later language development of J.J., and all other children who end up as native speakers, makes this abundantly clear.

However, once learnt, linguistic rules do seem to be automatically triggered. Using grammatical English seems to come naturally, although deciding on the content of what to insert into a syntactic 'frame' sometimes requires a lot of careful thought. Experts at day-to-day conversational exchanges, we can all be reduced to novices when we struggle to express our thoughts, fail to remember a spelling or are taken aback by realizing that we have misunderstood the structure of a sentence. For instance understanding the sense of *Read aloud the story sounds better* even changes our pronunciation of the letters *read*. This is the kind of sentence that would fox a beginner learning English, yet, after a moment's thought, it is quite comprehensible to expert speakers, a linguistic miracle indeed.

Conclusions

Below are listed some questions which reflect the many areas of our current ignorance about the knowledge and processes responsible for learning, acting and speaking.

1 What is the relation between declarative knowledge of facts and procedural knowledge of actions?
2 What are the processes by which factual knowledge becomes proceduralized into automatic production systems?
3 Can automatic procedures be monitored and adapted in the light of verbalized declarative representations?
4 Is language learned as a set of procedures for pairing conceptual meanings on to complete sentences, or is it more likely to result from matching simple 'child-like' utterances against objects and events in the environment?

10

Implications for teaching

The latest wave of cognitive learning theories have categorized teaching in a rather different way from past generations of psychologists. The metaphors of 'conditioning responses' and 'pouring information into memory stores' have been replaced by a new approach to learning. This asks the question: how can the world view of a novice be transformed into the world view of an expert? It is generally agreed that humans have an enormous amount of knowledge stored in memory about actions, probable consequences and the likely reactions of other people. The processes which enable us to understand language depend not only on knowing how to speak a language but also on the purposes of a conversation. Knowledge of objects which are eatable, rigid, dangerous, good for writing, represent just a tiny fraction of what we know about the world. From this pont of view most people can be thought of as experts in living, although even in this wide arena some people seem to have more expertise than others.

What is expertise?

The first question we need to address is what marks out special expertise from ordinary general knowledge? There are at least three ways of considering this question.

1 Experts have above average intelligence. This enables them to think and reason better than other people and to develop efficient general strategies for learning and problem-solving.
2 Experts have more factual knowledge about their own specific domain of expertise. Expertise is displayed in the ability to recognize and exploit relevant information within that domain.
3 Experts have developed automatic procedures for dealing with problems.

The difficulties of identifying pure intelligence are well known. However, it cannot be ruled out that more intelligent people – whatever it is that makes them so – are more likely to have the motivation to seek out expert knowledge. The ability to retrieve relevant information and to adjust it to the reality of incoming events is universally accepted as typical of expert performance. To the extent that expertise is proceduralized in Anderson's sense, routine sequences of behaviour can be run off automatically. The automatic nature of many low-level skills has been cited as evidence for innately wired-in input systems (Fodor, 1983). However, automaticity is also an acknowledged feature of expert skills which have obviously been learned, for example scientists recognizing proton traces, master chess players recognizing board positions, skilled writers producing strokes of the pen, and many other examples. The relationship between conscious factual knowledge and automatic skilled procedures is a topic which is more noted for its ubiquity in psychological theorizing than for convincing explanations. In this chapter I shall be considering attempts to teach people general thinking strategies, linguistic skills and expert knowledge.

Can thinking be taught?

Views about the possibility of improving people's ability to think intelligently depends on one's definition of intelligence.

Researchers like Eysenck (1986) and Jensen (1986) believe that each individual's intelligence is fixed by genetically based factors, which can be physiologically measured in terms of speed and accuracy of neural transmission. Not surprisingly, they offer little hope for the success of special improvement programmes, for example the Head Start initiative in the USA. However, even Eysenck and Jensen accept that experience has some effect on final performance levels. The bitter controversy between environmentalists and nativists concerns the amount of plasticity available for learning as opposed to strict upper limits on an individual's ability to benefit from education. This is the thinking behind statements that intelligence is due to 80 per cent inheritance, 20 per cent environment. The trouble with all such statements is that they assume that everyone starts off with an equal environment. If a child is extraordinarily deprived, shut up in an attic or an old-fashioned orphanage, alterations in environment will have a disproportionate effect. On the other hand, it could be that innately gifted people generate a more interesting environment for themselves, for example by reading books or tackling problems, which in turn increases their potential development (Pellegrino, 1986).

Most cognitive psychologists have paid little attention to possible causes of individual differences in intelligence. They are more interested in factors that are likely to affect cognitive processing in general. One suggestion that has emerged from the information processing framework (Simon, 1979) is that one of the main bottlenecks in processing information efficiently is the limited capacity of working memory. This is because task analysis and retrieval of appropriate problem-solving schemas has to take place in working memory. Studies of verbal reasoning and mental arithmetic have been carried out which demonstrate the strain these tasks put on working memory (Baddeley, 1986). Johnson-Laird (1983, 1985) attributed the failure of subjects to solve logical problems to limitations in working memory which prevent them from keeping track of mental models representing all possible counter-examples. It is the limit on the number of factors that can be considered simultaneously in working memory which makes thinking so hard. However, it is just as difficult to decide whether there are genetically determined differences in the biological hardware responsible for people having large or small working memory capacities as it is to isolate the role of genetic inheritance in other mental processes.

Whatever conclusion you come to about the biological basis for 'pure' intelligence, everyone agrees that there are many other cognitive and motivational factors which contribute to behaviour that is characterized as intelligent. To the extent that people differ in intelligent performance, which training strategies are most effective in fostering the ability to think constructively? One point on which there seems to be general agreement is that, the more problem-solving schemas are stored in long-term memory, the less likely it is that working memory will become overloaded. If people learn rules for solving logical problems, these can be run off without using up too much limited processing capacity. The belief in problem-solving strategies has led to training programs designed to train children to develop efficient strategies. One example is Meichenbaum's (1985) cognitive-behavioural training programme designed to enable children to gain control of cognitive strategies. The basic regime was for the child first to watch an adult model talking aloud while performing a task, then for the child to do the task following the adult's instructions, then for the child to perform the task alone but still talking aloud to itself, then with only silent self-instruction, until the child can perform the tasks automatically with no instructions at all, not even internalized verbalizations. This type of training has been applied in many different tasks, ranging from copying line drawings, and IQ tests, to eliminating cheating behaviour by schoolchildren. One important factor seems to be the adults' commentaries on their own actions, including articulating plans, congratulating themselves on their own success and suggesting remedies to correct errors. These draw the children's attention to their own methods of working, as well as providing a good model to follow.

This training programme has a lot in common with Anderson's (1983) model of gradually transforming verbalized declarative instructions into fully automatic procedures (although neither author quotes the other). Despite its behavioural emphasis, Meichenbaum's method of training children also has interesting parallels with Vygotsky's (1962) ideas about the gradual internalization of children's egocentric speech. Egocentric speech is so called because the child is essentially talking to itself, commenting on its own actions rather than attempting to communicate with other people. According to Vygotsky it is only around 6 or 7 that children finally learn to restrict overt language to those occasions when they want to communicate socially. At this age the use of language for monitoring and planning actions becomes internalized as inner speech, which takes on the role of thinking. This is just like the fourth stage of Meichenbaum's programme when the children carry out the behaviour without any overt verbalizations.

Teaching programmes of this kind aim to foster strategies which are designed to help children and students to modify and monitor their performance on all intellectual tasks. However, other researchers (Perkins, 1985) question the wisdom of attempting to teach general problem-solving strategies, pointing to the fact that most procedures are context-bound. The procedures used by experts for solving crossword puzzles or proving theorems in geometry are not likely to be much help with solving the Duncker radiation problem, much less writing an English essay. It may be useful to teach some general strategies, such as prior analysis of the task, perseverance in searching memory and checking evidence (Baron, 1985). Nevertheless Perkins and others argue that most skills need to be acquired through specific learning about a particular domain.

A reasonable conclusion is that even the teaching of general thinking strategies has to be related to a specific context, like line drawings or IQ tests. Novices find it difficult to select efficient strategies because they don't know enough about a domain to free their working memories from detailed consideration of the task in hand. Good chess players do not have to work out individual moves but can think in larger patterns. Skilled car drivers organize driving experiences into 'chunks' (Miller, 1956) such as 'turn right at the next junction' or 'emergency stop', whereas beginners have to solve the problem of pressing down the clutch and changing gear simultaneously. In Anderson's terms expert drivers have automatized these low-level skills as production systems in procedural memory. The main point of storing automatic procedures is to allow experts to pay attention to idiosyncratic events and the fine tuning of normally automatic skills. However, as Mandler (1985) argued, for teaching to be effective it must be possible for actions to be described, talked and thought about. It may be sensible, though, for teachers and textbook writers to try and take into account the stage of learning a student has reached, giving examples which will promote rapid proceduralization.

Of course, persuading people to think and to learn new problem-solving strategies also depends on motivational factors which have a profound effect on learning. The child who may be 'impulsive' when faced with an IQ test or a classroom task may take pains to become an expert on train spotting, mystery games or computing. At present no one claims to understand the relation between intelligence, learning and motivation in knowledge acquisition. It is instructive to note the comment by Goodnow (1986) that children – and adults – conform to the assessments made of them, playing up to the role of 'dumb' or 'smart' expected by teachers and friends, regardless of their 'natural' intelligence. On the other hand, the combination of intelligence and personal qualities that makes an individual stand out as a creative scientist or artist is equally a mystery.

Can language be taught?

The answer to this question will be very different depending on whether it is taken as referring to the original acquisition of a native language or to the later learning of second languages. It is the apparently effortless ease with which young children pick up the language around them (more than one language in a bilingual setting) which has led some researchers to propose an innate disposition for language learning. However, since each child is potentially capable of learning any language, the vocabulary and grammatical rules of each language must be learned. It was this paradox that led Chomsky to explain children's rapid ability to learn their native language in terms of linguistic universals which restrict the number of individual rules they have to learn. Chomsky's approach implies that children are born with the full panoply of abstract universal grammar biologically wired-in to their brains which equips them to learn the particular rules of their own language. On one level, this might be taken as saying no more than that the human brain has the innate potential to do all the things human beings are capable of, including walking, interacting with other people, understanding logic and talking. But Chomsky (1981) and his supporters go further in suggesting that there is a wired-in faculty for language which constitutes an actual, though tacit, knowledge of universal linguistic principles.

It would be foolish to imply that the mechanisms by which children learn a language are understood. The fact that virtually all children learn to talk – or in the case of deaf children develop other signal systems – argues in favour of a genetically based predisposition to learn human languages. On the other hand, it is sometimes forgotten that children do not achieve mastery of all the nuances of 'relevant' conversation until a much later age. Any adult who has tried to carry on a conversation with a small child will know how topics have to be tried out to test whether they fall within the child's knowledge and vocabulary. It is because children have not yet learned to anticipate shared knowledge and communicative intentions that conversations with young children can quickly run into the ground unless the adult takes the initiative in assessing the current state of the child's knowledge.

Adult speakers, too, differ greatly in their expressive command of a language, as revealed by a wide vocabulary and the selection of complex utterances to convey subtle meanings. It is an unresolved issue whether this is due to special linguistic abilities, general intelligence or familiarity with 'good' examples of language in conversations and books. As far as educators are concerned, exposure to examples of good usage seems to produce better results for linguistic fluency than direct teaching of grammatical skills. Environmentalists like Bernstein (1971) emphasize the importance of language use within the family. Motherese is a well-known term to describe the decisive importance of nonverbal and verbal interactions between infants and their caretakers. It is claimed that children who are given explanations when they ask questions develop a versatile use of language. This is, of course, a life-long process. As a teacher at the Open University, I have seen many instances of people learning new ways of using language to express ideas. It is, however, equally clear that the ability to use language for social communications, and to be sensitive to other speakers' intentions, has nothing to do with formal education.

When learning a second language it may be necessary to

practise vocabulary and grammar drill, but this is a poor substitute for the experience of a child being constantly surrounded by native speakers. This is the obvious reason why visiting the country concerned is considered to be an essential part of the learning process. The well-drilled language learner may know all the necessary vocabulary and grammar but still not know how to express meanings in an idiomatic way. Equally as important is the ability to select relevant speech acts in response to the commitments implied in conversational settings. It is hard enough to appreciate all the social and linguistic conventions within a single society. Sociolinguists have charted the pitfalls of literal translations which may have very different connotations, rude or vulgar, in other cultures. It is not at all easy to achieve just the right 'tone' in any unfamiliar situation, all the more difficult when using a different language in a different culture.

In a rather different context Winograd and Flores (1986) have developed a computerized 'communication co-ordinator', which is intended to improve the skills of people who need to communicate with colleagues in offices and business organizations by helping them to articulate explicitly the speech acts they intend to convey. The 'co-ordinator' presents people with a set of alternatives for structuring the content of their communications and specifying whether they are meant to be requests, commands, promises or acceptances. It also keeps track of what happens to these speech acts and whether they are fulfilled within a reasonable time-span. Although Winograd and Flores don't mention this as a possibility, it would be an interesting notion to adapt a co-ordinator of this kind to help foreign language students to select appropriate phrases for expressing speech acts, giving feedback in the language which is being taught.

One point that should be remembered is that, however well they learn to speak a language (unless at a very early age), second language learners tend to retain a strong foreign accent. This resistance to new accoustic patterns may be good evidence that low-level accoustic processing may be 'wired-in' to an early critical period for responding to the distinguishing sounds of a language. This would explain why acquiring a good accent is so recalcitrant to later learning. It is as if specific productions for pronunciation are locked away in procedural memory for ever. In fact it could plausibly be argued that understanding and producing language are among the earliest and best learnt automatic procedures we ever learn. Perhaps one reason why language learning appears to be so mysterious that it must have sprung Athena-like fully formed from the human brain is that there have been so many attempts to describe the incredibly complex rule system for producing and understanding all possible utterances. As I argued at the end of the previous chapter, children do not set themselves the task of learning grammatical rules. Instead they attend to the way utterances are used, at first to convey simple needs, later more complex occurrences and ideas. At the same time, language helps to extend their knowledge of the world. One implication for second language teaching is that learners, both children and adults, should be permitted to produce non-grammatical 'baby talk' utterances in their first attempts to express meanings in the new language, rather than to tackle straightaway the unrealistic task of being expected to produce complete sentences which are both grammatically correct and idiomatic.

Teaching facts or learning skills?

Despite all the difficulties encountered when trying to define intelligence, thinking and language, it is still possible to make some remarks about attempts to pass on expert knowledge to novices. It is a sobering thought that virtually all the education which goes on in schools, polytechnics and universities is confined to declarative knowledge about facts, as opposed to how to do things. It has been said of university lectures that information passes from the notes of the lecturer to the notes of the students without passing through the minds of either. The skills needed for doing maths problems or carrying out scientific experiments are typically taught by the teacher giving a demonstration from a position of superior expert knowledge, implying that there is a correct model which students must learn to copy. It has often been noted that the 'discovery learning' procedures found in primary schools are rarely carried over into secondary schools and university education.

In spite of the vast amount of information that is supposed to be transferred into the minds of students, many educationalists would agree that they do not know how to teach general skills, like taking well-structured notes, recognizing types of mathematical problems, testing experimental hypotheses, writing coherent essays and laboratory reports. These are just the kinds of skills that become automatic once they have been mastered. In all my years of university teaching, I am not all that optimistic about the effects of all the comments I have made on students' essays. The difficulty is to regain the viewpoint of someone who is a novice at skills which come so naturally to oneself. One definite drawback of the view of education as passing on a seamless web of expert knowledge is that teachers often cannot articulate tacit assumptions which might illuminate the underlying principles and goals of a topic. Their teaching has become routinized. Apart from the aimlessness and boredom this may cause among pupils, teachers are hardly ever faced with trouble-shooting situations which necessitate restructuring their own schemas. Despite the lip service that is paid to the proposition that people learn from errors, the process is such a painful one that teachers as well as pupils prefer to bypass it altogether.

Perhaps because of general dissatisfaction with teaching methods, there has been something of a shift towards more consideration of what is going on in the mind of the learner. It may be that some approaches to learning achieve better results than other learning styles. Studies of different cognitive learning styles by university students were reported by Richardson (1983). Richardson described the work of Marton (1976) and his colleagues at the University of Gothenburg in Sweden. This research emphasized a distinction between students who use 'deep-level processing' aimed at understanding the meaning of what they study, as opposed to 'surface-level processing', which focuses on reproducing the exact content of lectures and textbooks. There is evidence that students are consistent in their learning styles, as shown by the adverse effects of mismatching learning and teaching styles (Pask, 1976). It has also been shown that students adopt styles which they think are suited to the subject matter, and that they are influenced by the expectations of their teachers, and most crucially by their preconceptions about the way in which their work will be assessed and examined (Laurillard, 1979).

153

It is hard to wean students away from 'surface' rote learning if their syllabus is overloaded with facts and a display of factually correct knowledge is rewarded by their teachers. Research has shown that it is students whose intrinsic motivation impels them into 'deep' and holistic strategies for learning who actually do best in their final exams (Fransson, 1977). However, it is tempting for less motivated students to assume the opposite, which can lead to the phenomenon of 'knowledge-telling' in examinations, spilling out everything one knows about a topic without attempting to answer the question (Bereiter and Scardamalia, 1985). Carried to even further lengths, Norton and Hartley (1986) have demonstrated that one factor in successful examination performance is to 'retell' lecture notes, books and articles produced by the lecturer whom students believe is also going to mark the exam. Even if this is not the case, it is still a disheartening strategy for students to adopt.

A general survey of adults' attitudes to learning (Sälgö, 1979) indicated that most people assume that learning boils down to memorizing facts. Only a few individuals conceptualized learning as involving the possibility of different learning strategies according to the purpose and context of the learning required. The real problem is how to transform the student who believes in the teacher as an 'authority', who knows all the right answers, into a student who realizes that knowledge is available to anyone who searches for it (Perry, 1970). Some researchers imply that teachers should alter their teaching strategies to match those of their students. But it may be best for students pursuing rote learning strategies to be confronted by other demands, however alarming this may be in the first instance. This may all sound very pessimistic but there are, of course, many examples of students who have been inspired by their teachers to undertake independent study and research and have the motivation to master the skills required for acquiring and expressing knowledge. Undoubtedly, too, nearly everyone has some pet hobby or specialist topic about which they have acquired a lot of declarative facts and procedural knowledge.

Training for life?

The emphasis on learning facts in education is often unfavourably contrasted with the skills necessary for real life, including vocational skills. Employers, among others, claim that the declarative knowledge taught in schools and institutions of further education is not meeting the needs of society. Richardson (1983) quotes a revealing phrase to the effect that in academic learning the condition of 'strict understanding' is not enforced. The implication is that academics are playing at life. The skills of an airline pilot are, on the other hand, a matter of life and death. It is probably true to say that declarative knowledge of verbalized facts has had a very bad press both in education and cognitive psychology. Of course, the use of rote learning is rightly frowned on. However, verbalizations of facts, rules and principles is a different proposition altogether. For one thing, without declarative knowledge, what is there for proceduralization to get to work on? What makes teaching, and taking exams, so difficult is that we have to dredge up passive knowledge and make it active in an organized form in which it can be presented to others. Passing knowledge from one generation to the next depends on the ability of teachers, trainers and writers to articulate expertise and to communicate it to each new set of novices. But systematic communication is far from easy. Salesmen, therapists and interviewers may pre-plan verbal interactions, but this is stressful compared to normal conversations which flit about from topic to topic as we are reminded of one thing after another.

A final point to note is that experts can sometimes be almost too expert within a specific domain. The automatic activation of well-rehearsed problem-solving schemas may be a sign of mental laziness. Too tightly structured knowledge in relation to established goals may be inimical to new ideas. One definition of creativity refers to the ability to go beyond one's own expertise. It is not for nothing that children and other novices are credited with fresh insights. The true characterization of learning is the ability to cope with a range of experiences. The role of the expert teacher is to help the novice to exploit old experiences in interpreting and learning from new experiences.

11

Knowing and doing: what's it all about?

The intention of this chapter is to refer back to the main themes of the book, at the same time discussing them in relation to cognitive theories of human behaviour. In the first chapter I set out the following themes:

1 The central role of knowledge in interpreting the environment.
2 The process by which knowledge gets translated into speech and action.
3 The principles underlying the learning of facts and acts, strategies and procedures for action.

Throughout the intervening chapters we have come round full circle to these themes. None of them is ripe for solution but I hope that at least some issues have been clarified and relevant questions asked.

The role of knowledge in interpretation

The major function of knowledge depends on the ability to

retrieve relevant information as required. At any one point, the contents of active working memory are just the tip of the iceberg of all the information stored in passive memory. The memories we are reminded of, or consciously search for, seem to be a mishmash of general facts, half-remembered events and plans for dealing with current and future situations. The models of memory described in Chapters 3 and 4 are attempts to specify how knowledge stored in memory is represented and organized. The only general conclusion is that people's knowledge is so flexible that it can encompass hierarchies of categories (Collins and Quillian, 1969), typical instances and features (Rosch, 1975), frames for representing schemas (Minsky, 1975), scripts (Schank and Abelson, 1977), problem-solving schemas (Gick and Holyoak, 1980) and procedures for action (Anderson, 1983). In view of the multiplicity of knowledge structures in memory, a basic requirement is the recognition of similarities between previous experiences and new situations in order to appreciate the relevance of previously learned strategies and solutions to new problems. Examples are the appreciation of analogies which help to select appropriate problem-solving schemas (Gick and Holyoak, 1980) and the memory processes by which we are reminded of previous episodes (Schank, 1982). This assumes comparability between knowledge representations and the capability of switching from one framework to another, a process which has proved hard to model. Despite the general emphasis on reminding, the processes underlying the retrieval of knowledge representations and the fluctuating contents of working memory are beyond current psychological theories.

The issue of attempting to distinguish between different types of knowledge, semantic versus episodic (Tulving, 1972) and declarative versus procedural (Anderson, 1983) is also unresolved. Since it is impossible for all events to be remembered individually, the central dilemma is how general knowledge can be adapted to cope with the idiosyncratic nature of individual events. Yet it is obvious that knowledge representations play a crucial role in interpreting inputs and planning actions.

Knowledge and language

Many of the same problems arise in attempts to explain

how general knowledge and linguistic knowledge interact in interpreting individual utterances. One major issue raised in Chapter 5 is whether there is a need for a separate syntactic component for parsing the words in sentences into meaningful representations. The views range from those who believe that linguistic knowledge consists of syntactic rules and structures (Chomsky, 1957, 1965) to those who stress the importance of general knowledge (Schank and Abelson, 1977). It is undeniable that everyone has to refer to some syntactic rules to explain differences in meaning between *The man chased the dog*, *The dog chased the man*, *The cat was chased by the dog*, *Was the man chased by the dog*? But the attempt to specify a separate stage of syntactically derived literal meanings before applying general knowledge has run into difficulties. The semantic implausibility of *The mat sat on the cat* and *Flowers water girls* affects responses directly. Often syntactic analysis itself depends on knowledge of conceptual meanings, for example whether to treat *flies* as a verb or a noun in *Time flies like an arrow* and *Fruit flies like a banana*.

When it comes to using language for communication, general knowledge extends to the intentions of other people in making speech acts. Comprehension depends on mutual understanding between participants in verbal exchanges (Sperber and Wilson, 1986). Indeed one special characteristic of communication is that it inevitably involves other people. Language can be used to inform, to influence and to persuade, to convey emotions and to analyse motivations, to discuss decisions and to plan for the future. One of the characteristics of language is that it is a symbolic system which can be used to reflect upon reality, yet it can directly affect people's perception of the environment, including the actions of other people.

However, despite the 'meta' features of verbal communication, the issue of literal meanings cannot be entirely ignored. The possible range of meanings in a language one knows is a very different matter from the incomprehensible sounds of unfamiliar languages. And this linguistic knowledge seems to apply at all levels. It is possible to be drilled in the vocabulary of a foreign language without being able to string sentences together, to read a language but not to speak it, to be reduced to translating directly from one's own language or to speak fluently and idiomatically but with an atrocious accent, or to speak grammatically but to get the 'tone' wrong and so misunderstand speakers' intentions. There is an enormous, and largely unexplained, difference between just managing to order a meal in a foreign language and being able to chat and argue, joke and laugh, without being at any disadvantage among native speakers of another language.

Knowledge and action

Speech is, of course, one of the commonest of human actions. Yet the processes needed to turn knowledge into action have often been taken for granted in cognitive research. People's performance on memory tasks and evaluating sentences has been treated as evidence about how knowledge is organized rather than as being actions in their own right. The problem-solving schemas and procedural knowledge, formulated as productions in Anderson's (1983) theory have stimulated a new interest in theories of action, although mainly in the area of solving well-defined problems and puzzles. With simple problems like these it is possible to work out a problem space in which moves can be selected to work towards the solution of goals and subgoals or to trigger certain actions as a result of previous states of the problem (Newell and Simon, 1972). By conceptualizing problem-solving within an information processing framework (Simon, 1979), it is possible to mimic the performance of human solvers, as revealed by verbal protocols, by building in instructions for selecting the same moves into a computer program.

The major difficulty in modelling human problem-solving, especially when dealing with ill-defined problems in real life, is how to control actions towards achieving goals while at the same time allowing for flexible responsiveness to changing circumstances. Even if a perfect balance were to be achieved, it is all too clear that human beings are not able to formulate perfect strategies. This tension is shown in attempts to combine goal-directed means ends heuristics with working memory limitations (Atwood and Polson, 1976). The introduction of conflict resolution rules was another attempt to control the triggering of irrelevant actions. Too strict adherence to goals can restrict the ability to attend to more than one thing at a time or to monitor ongoing actions. Human experience seems to consist of a continual shifting between short-term and long-term goals (Neisser, 1986). A sign of a well-organized person is being able to keep track of the actions needed to achieve important goals.

Knowledge and learning

In the early years of psychology learning was a major topic and has, after many decades, again became an important area of study. The hallmark of the new theories is a move from the atomistic approach of the behaviourists to the realization that learners start off with a lot of prior knowledge which colours their response to new inputs. Anderson's (1983) model treated learning as a four-stage process: the absorption of declarative knowledge, the use of general problem-solving procedures to generate new productions, a proceduralization stage in which sequences of task-specific productions are compiled to run off independently of declarative memory, followed by a fine tuning of productions to deal with particular problem types.

Anderson's ACT attempts to model those aspects of expert performance which depend on the automatic recognition of input patterns. As demonstrated with chess players, mathematicians, readers and snooker players, this is an undoubted characteristic of experts in contrast to the laboured analysis of situations by novices. The ability to 'look up' procedures directly rather than to 'compute' them from first principles is a necessary condition for rapid expert performance. Nevertheless, while it is natural for teachers and trainers to wish to inculcate well-learned automatic skills, this approach plays down the role of language and thought in learning. Without the possibility of using language to monitor actions and to debate new procedures, behaviour would become routinized and teaching would be impossible. Human learning requires the ability to reconsider, and talk about, one's own actions in relation to those of an expert.

Thinking and attention

Ironically, thinking, with which I started the book, is often bypassed in theories of knowledge, learning and action. Perhaps this is because the aim is to build cognitive models, often as computer programs which, given a knowledge database and some processing rules, will automatically produce problem solutions and language interpretations. In fact thinking remains as elusive a concept as ever. In one sense, all the activities involved in speech and action can be defined as thinking; at other times, it seems that we speak and act before we think. Conscious thinking can be used for trying out alternative plans in the mind, bringing relevant knowledge into memory, shifting attention, and assessing whether an old procedure will do or whether more creative thought is required. When do new experiences fit into established knowledge structures? When are they so contradictory that they should be rejected as 'false'? When should old procedures and goals be abandoned altogether to be replaced by new goals? The existence of thinking as a mental activity mediating knowledge and action is attested by comments like 'keep quiet, I'm thinking'. Knowledge as belief systems, thinking as decision-making, control of action as attention shifts from one goal to another, these have all been described but are among the hardest problems of cognition to crack.

Norman (1980) went further in questioning the dependence of action on cognition. As shown in Figure 23 he gives pride of place to what he calls the 'regulatory system'. By this he means all the systems responsible for the survival of the species, paying attention to physical signals from the environment which require immediate action. The cognitive system is at the beck and call of the regulatory system, and is further confused by intrusions

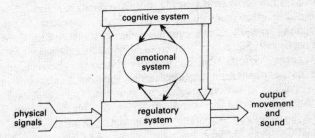

Figure 23 The regulatory system, the emotional system and the cognitive system.
Source: Norman (1980).

from the emotional system. Norman makes the point that it may be comforting for humans, and especially for cognitive psychologists, to think that a pure cognitive system is at the pinnacle of human functioning. Norman asks, 'Did the evolutionary sequence that produced superior cognitive systems do so to permit professors to exist, to publish, to hold conferences?' and answers himself, 'One suspects not, that the regulatory system was first, that the cognitive system grew out of the requirements of that system'.

The question which has to be considered is the purpose of human cognition. In a fight or flight situation, stopping to think may be catastrophic. This is neatly demonstrated by an amusing example by Fodor (1983). He quotes a couplet by Ogden Nash

> If you're called by a panther
> Don't anther

to demonstrate that, from the point of view of survival, it is important to have a fast visual response to a panther in your garden without needing to consult all the knowledge about panthers stored in memory. True enough. But how come we can recognize the meaning of the written letters *anther*? The fact that we do see the unexpected letter pattern is good evidence for the mandatory nature of reading letters once they have been learned. But it seems equally instantaneous to interpret this string of letters as *answer*, relying presumably on general knowledge about witty puns, interacting with syntactic and semantic linguistic knowledge. Quite apart from the advantages of appreciating poetry, it has to be said that the ability to cogitate about actions, to verbalize thinking, and to communicate the results of one's thinking to others, enables human action to transcend limitations of time and place and to avoid automatic responses to all situations. While the basic regulatory system may be a common evolutionary inheritance of the human species, the development of cognition encourages variation in individuals' responses to identical events. The overall structure of knowledge and the basic learning and processing mechanisms may be universal. But the contents of memory, based on personal experiences of facts and acts, is unique to each individual.

Human goals, for good or ill, go beyond instant survival. In the last resort it seems impossible to isolate all the different processes which contribute to human thinking and action. Attention to aspects of the perceived world are interpreted on the basis of past memories; thinking and language help to keep track of future plans and in turn direct attention to new events. Despite the apparent chaos of beliefs, prejudices, routine actions and conscious attempts to solve problems, humans are continually learning from experience. I can only hope that reading this book will add some useful, and usable, information to your current mental representations about memory, thinking and language.

Suggestions for further reading

General

Aitkenhead, A.M. and Slack, J.M. (eds) (1985) *Issues in Cognitive Modeling*, Hillsdale, NJ, Lawrence Erlbaum.

1 Introduction

Mandler, G. (1985) *Cognitive Psychology: An Essay in Cognitive Science*, Hillsdale, NJ, Lawrence Erlbaum.

2 Thinking and knowledge

Hudson, L. (1968) *Frames of Mind*, Harmondsworth, Penguin.
Sternberg, R.J. and Detterman, D.K. (eds) (1986) *What is Intelligence?* Norwood, NJ, Ablex.

3 The structure of knowledge

Roth, I. and Frisby, J.P. (1986) *Perception and Representation: A Cognitive Approach*, Milton Keynes, Open University Press.

4 Active memory

Cohen, G. Eysenck, M.W. and Le Voi, M.E. (1986) *Memory: A Cognitive Approach*, Milton Keynes, Open University Press.

Neisser, U. (ed.) (1982) *Memory Observed*, San Francisco, Calif., Freeman.

Schank, R.C. (1982) *Dynamic Memory*, Cambridge, Cambridge University Press.

5 Language and knowledge

Garnham, A. (1985) *Psycholinguistics: Central Topics*, London, Methuen.

Greene, J. (1986) *Language Understanding: A Cognitive Approach*, Milton Keynes, Open University Press.

Clark, H.H. and Clark, E.V. (1977) *Psychology and Language: An Introduction to Psycholinguistics*, New York, Harcourt Brace Jovanovich.

6 Language and communication

Ellis, A. and Beattie, G. (1986) *The Psychology of Language and Communication*, Hillsdale, NJ, Lawrence Erlbaum.

Sperber, D. and Wilson, D. (1986) *Relevance: Communication and Cognition*, Oxford, Blackwell.

Winograd, T. and Flores, F. (1986) *Understanding Computers and Cognition*, Norwood, NJ, Ablex.

8 Problem-solving

Kahney, H. (1986) *Problem Solving: A Cognitive Approach*, Milton Keynes, Open University Press.

9 Learning, acting and speaking

Anderson, J.R. (1983) *The Architecture of Cognition*, Cambridge, Mass., Harvard University Press.

10 Implications for teaching

Chipman, S.F., Segal, J.W. and Glaser, R. (eds) (1985) *Thinking and Learning Skills, Vol. 2*, Hillsdale, NJ, Lawrence Erlbaum.

Richardson, J.T.E. (1983) 'Student learning in higher education', *Educational Psychology*, 3, 305–31.

References and name index

Adelson, B. (1981) 'Problem solving and the development of abstract categories in programming languages', *Memory and Cognition*, 9, 422–33. *124*

Aitkenhead, A.M. and Slack, J.M. (eds) (1985) *Issues in Cognitive Modeling*, Hillsdale, NJ, Lawrence Erlbaum. *164*

Anderson, J.R. (1983) *The Architecture of Cognition*, Cambridge, Mass., Harvard University Press. *116, 118, 119, 129, 134, 140, 141, 147, 157, 159, 160, 165*

Argyle, M. (ed.) (1973) *Social Encounters*, Harmondsworth, Penguin. *86*

Armstrong, S.L., Gleitman, L.R. and Gleitman, H. (1983) 'What some concepts might not be', *Cognition*, 13, 263–308. *30*

Atwood, M.E., Masson, M.E.J. and Polson, P.G. (1980) 'Further explorations with a process model for water jug problems', *Memory and Cognition*, 8, 182–92. *109*

Atwood, M.E. and Polson, P.G. (1976) 'A process model for water jug problems', *Cognitive Psychology*, 8, 191–216. *109, 111, 159*

Austin, J.L. (1962) *How to Do Things with Words*, Oxford, Oxford University Press. *86*

Baddeley, A. (1986) *Working Memory*, Oxford, Clarendon Press. *39, 146*

Barber, P. (1987) *Applied Cognitive Psychology*, London, Methuen. *5, 55, 79*

Baron, J. (1985) 'What kinds of intelligence components are fundamental?', in S.F. Chipman, J.W. Segal and R. Glaser (eds) *Thinking and Learning Skills, Vol. 2*, Hillsdale, NJ, Lawrence Erlbaum. *11, 48*

Bartlett, F.C. (1932) *Remembering*, Cambridge, Cambridge University Press. *41, 42*

Bartlett, F.C. (1958) *Thinking*, New York, Basic Books. *113*

Bereiter, C. and Scardamalia, M. (1985) 'Cognitive coping strategies and the problem of inert knowledge', in S.F. Chipman, J.W. Segal and R. Glaser (eds) *Thinking and Learning Skills, Vol. 2*, Hillsdale NJ, Lawrence Erlbaum. *154*

Bernstein, B. (1971) *Class, Codes and Control, Vol. 1*, London, Routledge & Kegan Paul. *150*

Berwick, R.C. and Weinberg, A.S. (1984) *The Grammatical Basis of Linguistic Performance: Language Use and Acquisition*, Cambridge, Mass., MIT Press. *77*

Bever, T.G. (1970) 'The cognitive basis for linguistic structures', in J.R. Hayes (ed.) *Cognition and the Development of Language*, New York Wiley. *71*

Bower, G.H., Black, J.B. and Turner, T.J. (1979) 'Scripts in text comprehension and memory', *Cognitive Psychology*, 11, 177–220. *50, 53, 81*

Bransford, J.D., Barclay, J.R. and Franks, J.J. (1972) 'Sentence memory: a constructive versus interpretive approach', *Cognitive Psychology*, 3, 193–209. *80*

Bransford, J.D. and Franks, J.J. (1971) 'The abstraction of linguistic ideas', *Cognitive Psychology*, 2, 231–50. *82*

Bransford, J.D. and McCarrell, N.S. (1975) 'A sketch of a cognitive approach to comprehension: some thoughts about understanding what it means to comprehend', in W.B. Weimar and D.S. Palermo (eds) *Cognition and the Symbolic Processes*, Hillsdale, NJ, Lawrence Erlbaum. *80*

Brown, R. and Kulik, J. (1982) 'Flashbulb memories', in U. Neisser (ed.) *Memory Observed*, San Francisco, Calif., Freeman. *34*

Chase, W.G. and Simon, H.A. (1973) 'Perception in chess', *Cognitive Psychology*, 4, 55–81. *13, 120*

Chi, M.T.H., Feltovich, P.J. and Glaser, R. (1981) 'Categorization and representation of physics problems by experts and novices, *Cognitive Science*, 5, 121–52. *123, 128, 135*

Chipman, S.F., Segal, J.W. and Glaser, R. (eds) (1985) *Thinking and Learning Skills, Vol. 2*, Hillsdale, NJ, Lawrence Erlbaum. *166*

Chomsky, N. (1957) *Syntactic Structures*, The Hague, Mouton. *64, 68, 138*

Chomsky, N. (1959) 'Review of Skinner's *Verbal Behaviour*', *Language*, 35, 26–58. *63*

Chomsky, N. (1965) *Aspects of the Theory of Syntax*, Cambridge, Mass., MIT Press. *66, 67, 70, 73, 158*

Chomsky, N. (1981) *Lectures on Government and Binding*, Dordrecht, Holland, Foris Publications. *70, 83, 150*

Clark, H.H. (1977) 'Bridging', in P.N. Johnson-Laird and P.C. Wason (eds) *Thinking: Readings in Cognitive Science*, Cambridge, Cambridge University Press. *88, 89, 94*

Clark, H.H. and Clark, E.V. (1977) *Psychology and Language: An Introduction to Psycholinguistics*, New York, Harcourt Brace Jovanovich. *72*

Clark, H.H. and Murphy, G.L. (1982) 'Audience design in meaning and reference', in J.F. Le Ny and W. Kintsch (eds) *Language and Comprehension*, Amsterdam, North-Holland. *91*

Cohen, G., Eysenck, M.W. and Le Voi, M.E. (1986) *Memory: A Cognitive Approach*, Milton Keynes, Open University Press. *165*

Collins, A.M. and Loftus, E.F. (1975) 'A spreading-activation theory of semantic processing', *Psychological Review*, 82, 407–28. *25, 26*

Collins, A.M. and Quillian, M.R. (1969) 'Retrieval time from semantic memory', *Journal of Verbal Learning and Verbal Behaviour*, 8, 240–7. *19, 20, 21, 76, 157*

Collins, A.M. and Quillian, M.R. (1970) 'Does category size affect categorization time?', *Journal of Verbal Learning and Verbal Behaviour*, 9, 432–8. *25*

Conway, M.A. (1987) 'Verifying autobiographical facts', *Cognition*, 25, (in press). *35*

Conway, M.A. and Bekerian, D.A. (1987) 'Organisation in autobiographical memory', *Memory and Cognition*, 15, 119–32. *35*

de Groot, A.D. (1965) *Thought and Choice in Chess*, The Hague, Mouton. *13*

Duncker, K. (1945) 'On problem solving', *Psychological Monographs*, 58, 1–113. *8, 9, 10*

Ellis, A. and Beattie, G. (1986) *The Psychology of Language and Communication*, Hillsdale, NJ, Lawrence Erlbaum. *165*

Ewert, P.H. and Lambert, J.F. (1932) 'Part II: The effect of verbal instructions upon the formation of a concept', *Journal of General Psychology*, 6, 400–13. *123*

Eysenck, H.J. (1986) 'The theory of intelligence and the psychophysiology of cognition', in R.J. Sternberg (ed.) *Advances in the Psychology of Human Intelligence, Vol. 3*, Hillsdale, NJ, Lawrence Erlbaum. *146*

Fodor, J.A. (1983) *The Modularity of Mind*, Cambridge, Mass., MIT Press. *61, 97, 145, 162*

Fransson, A. (1977) 'On qualitative differences in learning: IV Effects of intrinsic motivation and extrinsic text anxiety on process and outcome', *British Journal of Educational Psychology*, 47, 244–57. *154*

Gahagan, J. (1984) *Social Interaction and its Management*, London, Methuen. *5, 86*

Garnham, A. (1985) *Psycholinguistics: Central Topics*, London, Methuen. *69, 165*

Getzels, J.W. and Jackson, P.W. (1963) 'The highly intelligent and the highly creative adolescent', in C.W. Taylor and F. Barron (eds) *Scientific Creativity: Its Recognition and Development*, New York, Wiley. *11*

Gick, M. and Holyoak, K.J. (1980) 'Analogical problem solving', *Cognitive Psychology*, 12, 306–56. Reprinted in A.M. Aitkenhead and J.M. Slack (eds) (1985) *Issues in Cognitive Modeling*, Hillsdale, NJ, Lawrence Erlbaum. *121, 122, 128, 157*

Goffman, E. (1971) *Relations in Public*, Harmondsworth, Penguin. *86*

Goodnow, J.J. (1986) 'A social view of intelligence', in R.J. Sternberg and D.K. Detterman (eds) *What is Intelligence?*, Norwood, NJ, Ablex. *149*

Greene, J. (1970) 'The semantic function of negatives and passives', *British Journal of Psychology*, 61, 17–22. *69*

Greene, J. (1986) *Language Understanding: A Cognitive Approach*, Milton Keynes, Open University Press. *74, 165*

Grice, H.P. (1975) 'Logic and conversation', in P. Cole and J.L. Morgan (eds) *Syntax and Semantics 3: Speech Acts*, New York, Academic Press. *88*

Guilford, J.P. (1959) 'Traits of creativity', in H.H. Anderson (ed.) *Creativity and Its Cultivation*, New York, Harper. *9*

Harris, J.E. (1984) 'Remembering to do things: a forgotten topic', in J.E. Harris and P.E. Morris (eds) *Everyday Memory, Actions and Absent-Mindedness*, London, Academic Press. *41*

Haviland, S.E. and Clark, H.H. (1974) 'What's new? Acquiring new information as a process in comprehension', *Journal of Verbal Learning and Verbal Behaviour*, 13, 512–21. *90*

Hayes, J.R. and Simon, H.A. (1974) 'Understanding written problem instructions', in L.W. Gregg (ed.) *Knowledge and Cognition*, Hillsdale, NJ, Lawrence Erlbaum. *122*

Herriot, P. (1969) 'The comprehension of active and passive sentences as a function of pragmatic expectations', *Journal of Verbal Learning and Verbal Behaviour*, 8, 166–9. *69*

Hitch, G.J. (1978) 'The role of short-term working memory in mental arithmetic', *Cognitive Psychology*, 10, 302–23. *39*

Horn, J. (1986) 'Intellectual ability concepts', in R.J. Sternberg (ed.) *Advances in the Psychology of Human Intelligence, Vol. 3*, Hillsdale, NJ, Lawrence Erlbaum. *11*

Hudson, L. (1968) *Frames of Mind*, Harmondsworth, Penguin. *11, 164*

Jensen, A.R. (1986) 'Intelligence: "definition", measurement and future research', in R.J. Sternberg and D.K. Detterman (eds) *What is Intelligence?*, Norwood, NJ, Ablex. *146*

Johnson-Laird, P.N. (1983) *Mental Models*, Cambridge, Cambridge University Press. *146*

Johnson-Laird, P.N. (1985) 'Logical thinking: does it occur in daily life? Can it be taught?, in S.F. Chipman, J.W. Segal and R. Glaser (eds) *Thinking and Learning Skills, Vol. 2*, Hillsdale, NJ, Lawrence Erlbaum. *146*

Johnson-Laird, P.N. and Stevenson, R. (1970) 'Memory for Syntax', *Nature*, 227, 412. *81*

Johnson-Laird, P.N. and Wason, P.C. (eds) (1977) *Thinking: Readings in Cognitive Science*, Cambridge, Cambridge University Press. *45*

Kahney, H. (1986) *Problem Solving: A Cognitive Approach*, Milton Keynes, Open University Press. *103, 108, 165*

Katona, G. (1940) *Organising and Memory*, New York, Hafner. *8, 18*

Kimball, J. (1973) 'Seven principles of surface structure parsing in natural language', *Cognition*, 2, 15–47. *71*

Labov, W. (1973) 'The boundaries of words and their meanings', in C.J. Bailey and R. Shuy (eds) *New Ways of Analysing Variations in English*, Washington, DC, Georgetown University Press. *32*

Laurillard, D. (1979) 'The process of student learning', *Higher Education*, 8, 395–409. *153*

Linton, M. (1982) 'Transformations of memory in everyday life', in U. Neisser (ed.) *Memory Observed*, San Francisco, Calif., Freeman. *33*

Mandler, G. (1985) *Cognitive Psychology: An Essay in Cognitive Science*, Hillsdale, NJ, Lawrence Erlbaum. *2, 40, 137, 148, 164*

Marton, F. (1976) 'What does it take to learn? Some implications of an alternative view of learning', in N. Entwistle (ed.) *Strategies for Research and Development in Higher Education*, Amsterdam, Swets & Zeitlinger. *153*

Meichenbaum, D. (1985) 'Teaching thinking: a cognitive-behavioral perspective', in S.F. Chipman, J.W. Segal and R. Glaser (eds) *Thinking and Learning Skills, Vol. 2*, Hillsdale, NJ, Lawrence Erlbaum. *147*

Miller, G.A. (1956) 'The magical number seven plus or minus two: some limits on our capacity for processing information', *Psychological Review*, 63, 81–97. *148*

Miller, G.A. and McKean, K.O. (1964) 'A chronometric study of some relations between sentences', *Quarterly Journal of Experimental Psychology*, 16, 297–308. *68*

Minsky, M. (1975) 'A framework for representing knowledge', in

P. Winston (ed.) *The Psychology of Computer Vision*, New York, McGraw-Hill. *43, 48, 54, 157*

Neisser, U. (1976) *Cognition and Reality*, San Francisco, Calif., Freeman. *55, 56*

Neisser, U. (ed.) (1982) *Memory Observed*, San Francisco, Calif., Freeman. *34, 165*

Neisser, U. (1986) 'Nested structure in autobiographical memory', in D.C. Rubin (ed.) *Autobiographical Memory*, Cambridge, Cambridge University Press. *125, 136, 160*

Neves, D.M. and Anderson, J.R. (1981) 'Knowledge compilation: mechanisms for the automatization of cognitive skills', in J.R. Anderson (ed.) *Cognitive Skills and their Acquisition*, Hillsdale, NJ, Lawrence Erlbaum. *138*

Newell, A. (1973) 'Production systems: models of control structures', in W.G. Chase (ed.) *Visual Information Processing*, New York, Academic Press. *112*

Newell, A. and Simon, H.A. (1972) *Human Problem Solving*, Englewood Cliffs, NJ, Prentice-Hall. *106, 113, 159*

Nisbett, R.E. and Wilson, T.D. (1977) 'Telling more than we can know: verbal reports on mental processes', *Psychological Review*, 84, 231–59. *105*

Norman, D.A. (1980) 'Twelve issues for cognitive science', *Cognitive Science*, 4, 1–33. Reprinted in A.M. Aitkenhead and J.M. Slack (eds) (1985) *Issues in Cognitive Modeling*, Hillsdale, NJ, Lawrence Erlbaum. *161*

Norman, D.A. (1981) 'Categorization of action slips', *Psychological Review*, 88, 1–15. *125*

Norton, L.S. and Hartley, J. (1986) 'What factors contribute to good examination marks?', *Higher Education*, 15, 355–71. *154*

Olson, D.R. (1970) 'Language and thought: aspects of a cognitive theory of semantics', *Psychological Review*, 77, 257–73. *29*

Parsons, D. (1969) *Funny Amusing and Funny Amazing*, London, Pan. *88*

Pask, G. (1976) 'Styles and strategies of learning', *British Journal of Educational Psychology*, 46, 128–48. *11, 153*

Pellegrino, J. W. (1986) 'Intelligence: the interaction of culture and cognitive processes', in R.J. Sternberg and D.K. Detterman (eds) *What is Intelligence?*, Norwood, NJ, Ablex. *146*

Perkins, D.N. (1985) 'General cognitive skills: why not?, in S.F. Chipman, J.W. Segal and R. Glaser (eds) *Thinking and Learning Skills, Vol. 2*, Hillsdale, NJ, Lawrence Erlbaum. *148*

Perry, W.G. jun. (1970) *Forms of Intellectual and Ethical Development in the College Years: A Scheme*, New York, Holt, Rinehart & Winston. *154*

Reason, J.T. (1979) 'Actions not as planned: the price of automatization', in G. Underwood and R. Stevens (eds) *Aspects of Consciousness*, Vol. *1*, New York, Academic Press. *40*

Reed, S.K., Ernst, G.W. and Banerji, R. (1974) 'The role of analogy in transfer between similar problem states', *Cognitive Psychology*, 6, 436–50. *122*

Richardson, J.T.E. (1983) 'Student learning in higher education', *Educational Psychology*, 3, 305–31. *153, 155, 166*

Rosch, E. (1973) 'On the internal structure of perceptual and semantic categories', in T.E. Moore (ed.) *Cognitive Development and the Acquisition of Language*, New York, Academic Press. *30*

Rosch, E. (1975) 'Cognitive representations of semantic categories', *Journal of Experimental Psychology: General*, 104, 192–233. *26, 27, 157*

Rosch, E. (1978) 'Principles of categorization', in E. Rosch and B.B. Lloyd (eds) *Cognition and Categorization*, New York, Wiley. *27*

Rosch, E., Mervis, C.B., Gray, W.D., Johnson, D.M. and Boyes-Graem, P. (1976) 'Basic objects in natural categories', *Cognitive Psychology*, 8, 382–439. *28, 29*

Roth, I. (1986) 'Conceptual categories', in I. Roth and J.P. Frisby, *Perception and Representation: A Cognitive Approach*, Milton Keynes, Open University Press. *31*

Roth, I. and Frisby, J.P. (1986) *Perception and Representation: A Cognitive Approach*, Milton Keynes, Open University Press. *165*

Rumelhart, D.E. and Norman, D.A. (1983) *Representation in Memory: CHIP Technical Report (no 116)*, San Diego, Calif., Center for Human Information Processing, University of California. Reprinted in A.M. Aitkenhead and J.M. Slack (eds) (1985) *Issues in Cognitive Modeling*, Hillsdale, NJ, Lawrence Erlbaum. *131*

Sachs, J.S. (1967) 'Recognition memory for syntactic and semantic aspects of connected discourse', *Perception and Psychophysics*, 2, 437–42. *81*

Sälgö, R. (1979) 'Learning about learning', *Higher Education*, 8, 443–51. *154*

Sanford, A.J. (1985) *Cognition and Cognitive Psychology*, Hillsdale, NJ, Lawrence Erlbaum.

Schank, R.C. (1972) 'Conceptual dependency: a theory of natural language understanding', *Cognitive Psychology*, 3, 552–631. *77*

Schank, R.C. (1982) *Dynamic Memory*, Cambridge, Cambridge University Press. *40, 52, 157, 165*

Schank, R.C. and Abelson, R.P. (1977) *Scripts, Plans, Goals and Understanding*, Hillsdale, NJ, Lawrence Erlbaum. *49, 51, 157, 158*

Schank, R.C. and the Yale AI Project (1975) *SAM: A Story Understander*, Research Report 43, New Haven, Conn., Yale University Department of Computer Science. *74*

Searle, J.R. (1969) *Speech Acts*, Cambridge, Cambridge University Press. *86*

Shackleton, V. and Fletcher, C. (1984) *Individual Differences*, London, Methuen. *5, 7*

Simon, H.A. (1975) 'The functional equivalence of problem solving skills', *Cognitive Psychology*, 7, 268–88. *118, 123*

Simon, H.A. (1979) 'Information-processing theory of human problem solving', in W. Estes (ed.) *Handbook of Learning and Cognitive Processes*, *Vol. 5*, Hillsdale, NJ, Lawrence Erlbaum. Reprinted in A.M. Aitkenhead and J.M. Slack (eds) (1985) *Issues in Cognitive Modeling*, Hillsdale, NJ, Lawrence Erlbaum. *105, 106, 107, 114, 119, 146*

Skinner, B.F. (1957) *Verbal Behaviour*, New York, Appleton-Century-Crofts. *62*

Slobin, D.I. (1966) 'Grammatical transformations and sentence comprehension in childhood and adulthood', *Journal of Verbal Learning and Verbal Behaviour*, 5, 219–27. *69*

Smith, E.E., Shoben, E.J. and Rips, L.J. (1974) 'Structure and process in semantic memory: a featural model for semantic decisions', *Psychological Review*, 81, 214–41. *24, 26*

Sperber, D. and Wilson, D. (1986) *Relevance: Communication and Cognition*, Oxford, Blackwell. *92, 94, 158, 165*

Sternberg, R.J. and Detterman, D.K. (eds) (1986) *What is Intelligence?* Norwood, NJ, Ablex. *164*

Trudgill, P. (1974) *Sociolinguistics*, Harmondsworth, Penguin. *86*

Tulving, E. (1972) 'Episodic and semantic memory' in E. Tulving and W. Donaldson (eds) *Organization of Memory*, New York, Academic Press. *32, 157*

Turner, J. (1984) *Cognitive Development and Education*, London, Methuen. *5*

Vygotsky, L.S. (1962) *Thought and Language*, Cambridge, Mass., MIT Press. *60, 147*

Wason, P.C. (1965) 'The context of plausible denial', *Journal of Verbal Learning and Verbal Behaviour*, 4, 7–11. *69*

Weizenbaum, J. (1966) 'ELIZA – a computer program for the study of natural language', *Communications of the Association for Computing Machinery*, 9, 36–45. *74*

Winograd, T. (1972) *Understanding Natural Language*, New York, Academic Press. *74, 94*

Winograd, T. (1980) 'What does it mean to understand language?', *Cognitive Science*, 4, 209–41. Reprinted in A.M. Aitkenhead and J.M. Slack (eds) (1985) *Issues in Cognitive Modeling*, Hillsdale, NJ, Lawrence Erlbaum. *94, 95*

Winograd, T. and Flores, F. (1986) *Understanding Computers and Cognition*, Norwood, NJ, Ablex. *94, 95, 151, 165*

Subject index

ACT (Adaptive Control
   Theory), 129, 137
active memory, 37–40
algorithms, 107, 120
analogies, 15, 121–2
analysis by synthesis, 56
artificial intelligence, 73, 94,
   106
attention, 160–1
audience design, 91
autobiographical facts, 35
autobiographical memories,
   34–5

basic-level categories, 28–9
bottom-up processing, 54
box and arrow models, 3
bridging inferences, 88–90

categories, 19
characteristic features, 23–5
chess, 13, 119–20, 133
cognition, 2
cognitive architecture, 118
cognitive economy, 22, 45, 53,
   76
cognitive psychology, 1–3
cognitive styles, 11
cognitive-behavioural training,
   147
Collins and Quillian network,
   20–2, 43, 48, 130
communication, 85
communicative intentions, 92
computer models of problem-
   solving, 105–13
conation, 2

concepts, 17, 19–22
conflict resolution rules, 115–18, 134
convergent thinking, 11
creativity, 11, 124, 155
cryptarithmetic problems, 113–15

database, 3, 19–20, 105
declarative knowledge, 129, 137, 155
declarative memory, 129–34, 137
deep structures, 66–7, 71
default values, 45–8, 84
defining features, 19, 22–6, 30
discourse analysis, 79
divergent thinking, 11
Duncker's radiation problem, 8–10, 121
dynamic memory, 53

education, 152–5
egocentric speech, 147
emotion, 2, 161–2
episodic memory, 32–5, 53, 130
event memory, 53
expertise, 120, 145, 155
experts, 5, 14–15, 120, 123–4, 128, 138, 145, 148, 155

feature comparison models, 23–5, 30
felicity conditions, 87
flashbulb memories, 34
frames, 43–52, 77–8, 83

free recall, 19
Freud, 34, 37
fuzzy concepts, 27

General Problem Solver (GPS), 106–7, 118
Gestalt laws, 8
goals, 52, 108, 117, 136

heuristic strategies, 107

indirect speech acts, 87
inferential explosion, 48, 51
information processing, 3, 106, 146
inheritance, 22, 45
input representations, 55, 122
insight, 8
intelligence, 7, 12, 145–7

knowledge, 1, 4, 11–15, 17–18, 37, 61, 119, 156
knowledge-based inferences, 79
knowledge compilation, 135
Koffka, 8
Kohler, 8

language, 59–61, 138–42, 149–52
language acquisition, 63, 83–4, 140–2, 149–52
language productions, 138–9
learning, 128–9, 133–4, 137–8, 144, 152–6

learning styles, 153–4
levels of problem-solving,
    12–13, 120
linguistic competence, 67, 70
linguistic relativity hypothesis,
    60
linguistic rules, 63, 139–40
linguistic universals, 70, 83,
    142, 149
literal meaning, 87, 97
long-term memory, 4, 39, 129

means ends analysis, 107–11,
    117, 137
memory organization packets
    (MOPs), 53
memory stores, 3, 33, 38, 137
mental lexicon, 76–8
mental models, 146
Missionaries and Cannibals,
    109–10
mnemonics, 38
modularity, 113
motherese, 150
motivational factors, 125, 149
mutual knowledge, 91

natural language
    understanding programs,
    73–4, 77
novices, 5, 15, 120, 123–4,
    128, 133, 148, 152, 155

object recognition, 24, 31,
    54–6
optimal relevance, 93

parsing strategies, 71–3
passive memory, 37–8, 155,
    157
pattern matching, 55, 132
perceptual cycle, 56
performative utterances, 86
personal memories, 35
phrase structure rules, 64, 67
Piaget, 2
pragmatics, 86
problem space, 106, 122–3
problem-solving, 8, 103–4
problem-solving schemas,
    120–3, 137, 147, 155
procedural learning, 133–6,
    138
procedural memory, 129–35,
    137
proceduralization, 135, 138,
    149
production systems, 112–18,
    132–5, 139, 142
productions, 112–19, 132–8
prospective memory, 41
prototypes, 27
psycholinguistic experiments,
    68–71
psychometrics, 6

recognition confusions, 80–1
relevance, 92
reminding, 40, 52, 54–5
restaurant script, 49–51, 55
retrospective memory, 41
rote learning, 154–5

Sapir-Whorf hypothesis, 59
schemas, 41–8, 53–4, 56

scripts, 49–53, 78
second language learning,
  150–2
secondary representations,
  137
semantic component, 66
semantic knowledge, 33–6,
  130
semantic memory, 32–3
semantic network, 19
sentence verification, 21,
  68–70
short-term memory, 39
skills, 135, 137–8, 152–5
speech acts, 86–7, 94–6, 151
subgoals, 108, 117, 136
surface structures, 66–8
symbolic representations, 3
syntactic component, 67
syntactic rules, 64, 140

Teachable Language
  Comprehender (TLC), 19
teaching, 144, 148, 152–3
thinking, 6–7, 145, 160
top-down processing, 54

Tower of Hanoi, 105–6, 109,
  118, 122–3
training, 147, 154
transfer effects, 122
transformational grammar,
  63–4, 70
transformational rules, 66, 70
typicality, 26–7, 30

universal grammar, 83, 149

verbal protocols, 9, 105–6,
  123, 135
verbal responses, 61–2

War of the Ghosts story, 42,
  82
waterjug problems, 109–11
Wertheimer, 8
word meanings, 75–7
working memory, 39–40,
  110–11, 120, 132, 134–5,
  146–7, 157